PEARSON

my Student JOURNAL

This Student Journal belongs to

_____

PEARSON

Boston, Massachusetts
Chandler, Arizona
Glenview, Illinois
Upper Saddle River, New Jersey

Acknowledgments appear on page 182, which constitute an extension of this copyright page.

ISBN-13:   978-0-13-363806-6
ISBN-10:   0-13-363806-5
20   18

How to Use This Book

The *myWorld Geography Student Journal* is a tool to help you process and record what you have learned from the Student Edition of *myWorld Geography*. As you complete the activities and essays in your Journal, you will be creating your own personal resource for reviewing the concepts, key terms, and maps from *myWorld Geography*. The Journal worksheets and writing exercises focus on the Essential Question, helping you uncover the relevance of each chapter to your life.

The **Essential Question Preview** will help you understand the chapter you are about to read. Begin with Connect to Your Life to find ways to relate the issues and principles of the Essential Questions to your life—your family, school, or community. Next, Connect to the Chapter invites you to flip through the chapter and chart your predictions on how the Essential Question relates to the countries in each chapter.

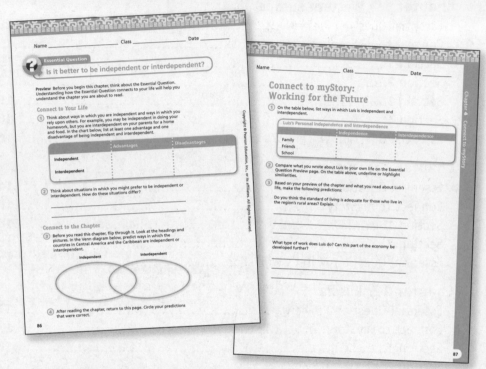

You will build your Map Skills and make the maps your own by locating features on the line maps in **Take Notes.** You can synthesize concepts and create a detailed visual study guide by filling in the illustrated graphic organizers in Take Notes. Each Take Notes page ends with an exercise that helps you draw conclusions about the Essential Question.

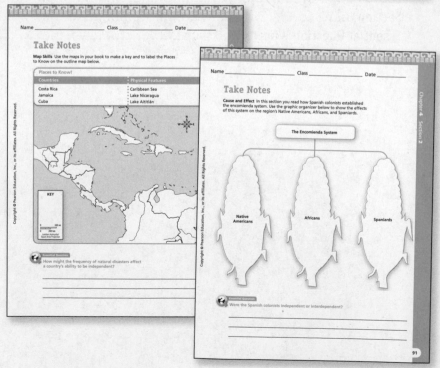

Name _____ Class _____ Date _____

Essential Question Writer's Workshop

Is it better to be independent or interdependent?

Prepare to Write

Throughout this chapter, you have explored the Essential Question in your text, journal, and On Assignment at myWorldGeography.com. Using what you have learned, write an essay in which you explain whether it is better for Central American and Caribbean nations to be independent or interdependent.

Workshop Skill: Write an Introduction and Thesis Statement

First, review the four types of essays. Then decide which type is best suited to the ideas you wish to express. Which type of essay have you chosen?

_____

Develop your thesis, which is your response to the Essential Question. Begin by reviewing your notes. To help you choose a position, list reasons that support each position in the table below.

Independent	Interdependent

Write the position you have chosen below, along with the three strongest reasons that support it. Note at least one fact or example for each reason.

Position	
Supporting Reasons	Facts and/or Examples

Write Your Thesis Statement

Your thesis statement states your position and three reasons that support it. The thesis statement will be the last sentence(s) in your introductory paragraph. For example: *Independence is essential for Central American and Caribbean nations because*

_____ and _____.

If your sentence is too long, place your reasons in a second sentence. For example: *Independence is essential for Central American and Caribbean countries. This is true because*

_____ and _____.

Now write your thesis statement:

_____

Write Your Introduction

The first paragraph of an essay introduces the topic to the reader. An introduction has three parts:

1. A statement indicating what the essay is about.

Example *Independence and interdependence are characteristics that*

_____

2. An indication of why the subject or issue is important.

Example *Understanding a particular nation's independence or interdependence is essential to understanding* _____

3. A thesis statement.

Write your introductory sentence: _____

State the issue's importance: _____

Write your thesis statement, including three supporting arguments: _____

Draft Your Essay

Introduction: Rewrite your introductory paragraph on your own paper.
Body Paragraphs: Develop each argument to support your position in a separate paragraph. Include details and examples.
Conclusion: Summarize your arguments. When you have finished, proofread your essay.

94   95

The **Essential Question Writer's Workshop** provides you an end-of-chapter opportunity to show your understanding of chapter content by writing about the Essential Question. Each Workshop features instruction and practice with one of the skills you will need to write an essay and express your ideas. The Writer's Workshop exercises and the activities you have completed in your Journal will help you draw conclusions about the Chapter Essential Question.

The **Word Wise** exercises give you the chance to really get to know and explore the key terms through word maps, crossword puzzles, and other game formats.

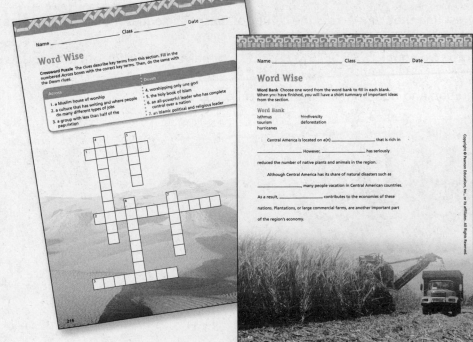

Name _____ Class _____ Date _____

Word Wise

Crossword Puzzle The clues describe key terms from this section. Fill in the numbered Across boxes with the correct key terms. Then, do the same with the Down clues.

Across
1. a Muslim house of worship
2. a culture that has writing and where people do many different types of jobs
3. a group with less than half of the population

Down
4. worshipping only one god
5. the holy book of Islam
6. an all-powerful leader who has complete control over a nation
7. an Islamic political and religious leader

216

Name _____ Class _____ Date _____

Word Wise

Word Bank Choose one word from the word bank to fill in each blank. When you have finished, you will have a short summary of important ideas from the section.

Word Bank
isthmus
tourism
hurricanes
biodiversity
deforestation

Central America is located on a(n) _____ that is rich in _____ However, _____ has seriously reduced the number of native plants and animals in the region.

Although Central America has its share of natural disasters such as _____ many people vacation in Central American countries. As a result, _____ contributes to the economies of these nations. Plantations, or large commercial farms, are another important part of the region's economy.

1

Core Concepts 1.1: Word Wise

Word Bank Choose one word from the word bank to fill in each blank.
When you have finished, you will have a short summary of important ideas
from the section.

Word Bank

geography	cardinal directions
sphere	latitude
degrees	longitude
hemispheres	

North, south, east, and west are the _____. People use

them to describe the location of places. They also use imaginary lines drawn

across the surface of Earth. Lines that run north to south are called lines of

_____, while those that run east to west are lines of

_____. These lines are measured in units called

_____. Each one of these lines goes in a circle around Earth,

which has the shape of a _____. The equator is the east-

west line that runs across the center of Earth. The equator divides our planet

into two equal _____, or halves. The study of Earth and its

human and non-human features is called _____.

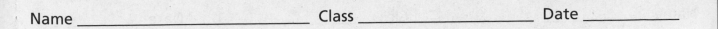

Name _____ Class _____ Date _____

Core Concepts 1.2: Word Wise

Words In Context For each question below, write an answer that shows your understanding of the boldfaced key term.

(1) How does **absolute location** differ from **relative location**?

_____

_____

(2) What does the geographic theme of **place** describe about a location?

_____

_____

(3) The Midwest is one **region** of the United States. What characteristics make it a region?

_____

_____

(4) How can you see the theme of **movement** in a city like Washington, D.C.?

_____

_____

(5) How does **human-environment interaction** affect your life?

_____

_____

Core Concepts 1.3: Word Wise

Vocabulary Quiz Show Some quiz shows ask a question and expect the contestant to give the answer. In other shows, the contestant is given an answer and must supply the question. If the blank is in the question column, write the question that would result in the answer given. If the question is supplied, write the appropriate answer.

QUESTION	ANSWER
1 What do you call photographs taken from airplanes or helicopters?	**1** _____
2 _____	**2** scale
3 What is the name for a computer-based system that stores and uses information linked to geographic locations?	**3** _____
4 _____	**4** satellite images
5 What do you call a flat map of Earth's round surface?	**5** _____
6 _____	**6** distortion

Name _____ Class _____ Date _____

Core Concepts 1.4: Word Wise

Crossword Puzzle The clues describe key terms from this section. Fill in the
numbered *Across* boxes with the correct key terms. Then, do the same with
the *Down* clues.

Across	Down
1. a map that shows a larger area than the main map	4. a standard map diagram that shows the cardinal directions
2. the map part that shows how much space on the map represents a given distance	
3. the map part that shows what the map symbols mean	

Core Concepts 1.5: Word Wise

Sentence Builder Complete the sentences using the information you learned in this section. Be sure to include terminal punctuation.

(1) **Elevation** refers to the _____

_____

_____

(2) A **special-purpose map** may show such things as _____

_____

_____

(3) A **political map** of your state would show _____

_____

_____

(4) A **physical map** shows _____

_____

_____

Name _____ Class _____ Date _____

Sum It Up

Map Your Classroom Apply what you have learned about the tools of geography to your life by drawing a map of your classroom. Include a key and a compass rose. Use a tape measure or yardstick to make a scale bar. Draw a locator map to show the location of your classroom within your school.

Use the theme of place to describe the relative location of your classroom.

_____

_____

_____

Core Concepts 2.1: Word Wise

Sentence Builder Complete the sentences using the information you learned in this section. Include terminal punctuation.

(1) Earth moves around the sun in an **orbit** that takes _____

days to _____

(2) The months of _____ and _____ have

the _____ and _____ **equinoxes**,

which are _____

(3) It takes Earth _____ to complete a **revolution**, which is

_____

(4) The _____ and _____ **solstices**, which

occur during the months of _____ and

_____, are _____

(5) Earth _____ on its **axis**, which is an imaginary

_____

Name _____ Class _____ Date _____

Core Concepts 2.2: Word Wise

Words In Context For each question below, write an answer that shows your understanding of the boldfaced key term.

1 How does Earth's **rotation** differ from its revolution?

_____

_____

_____

2 Why does Earth have multiple **time zones**?

_____

_____

_____

Core Concepts 2.3: Word Wise

Vocabulary Quiz Show Some quiz shows ask a question and expect the contestant to give the answer. In other shows, the contestant is given an answer and must supply the question. If the blank is in the question column, write the question that would result in the answer given. If the question is supplied, write the appropriate answer.

QUESTION	ANSWER
(1) _____	(1) core
(2) What do you call the thick layer of gases that surround our planet and make life possible?	(2) _____
(3) _____	(3) mantle
(4) What gets created by the physical processes that change Earth's surface by pushing its crust up or wearing it down?	(4) _____
(5) _____	(5) crust

Core Concepts 2.4: Word Wise

Crossword Puzzle The clues describe key terms from this section. Fill in the numbered *Across* boxes with the correct key terms. Then, do the same with the *Down* clues.

Across

1. when water, ice, or wind remove small pieces of rock
2. a stretch of low land between mountains, often formed by a river
3. occurs when running water picks up material from one place and leaves it in another
4. a high area with a flat top and at least one steep side

Down

5. flat plains formed on the seabed where a river deposits material over many years
6. a large area of flat or gently rolling land
7. wearing down rocks by chemical or mechanical means

Core Concepts 2.5: Word Wise

Word Bank Choose one word from the word bank to fill in each blank. When you have finished, you will have a short summary of important ideas from the section.

Word Bank

magma   plates
faults   plate tectonics

Earth's crust is broken up into many huge blocks called

_____. According to the theory of _____,

these blocks slide and grind against one another. The places where their

edges meet are called _____, and this is where volcanoes

often form. When a volcano erupts, _____, which is melted

rock from deep within Earth, pours out onto the crust. Once it comes out of

the volcano, it is called lava.

Name _____ Class _____ Date _____

Sum It Up

Label the Diagram Mark these physical features in the appropriate areas on the diagram below.

river valley   plateau

delta   mountains

Name three forces that create these features. Explain how each one works.

_____

_____

_____

Name _____ Class _____ Date _____

Core Concepts 3.1: Word Wise

Sentence Builder Complete the sentences using the information you learned in this section. Include terminal punctuation.

1 Types of **precipitation** include _____

_____

2 **Climate** describes the average _____ and other factors in

an area _____

3 Listening to a **weather** forecast lets you know _____

_____

4 On a climate graph, the line labeled **temperature** shows _____

_____

Core Concepts 3.2: Word Wise

Crossword Puzzle The clues describe key terms from this section. Fill in the numbered *Across* boxes with the correct key terms. Then, do the same with the *Down* clues.

Across	Down
1. name for the areas that lie north of the Arctic Circle and south of the Antarctic Circle	5. height above sea level
2. term describing the area between high and low latitudes	6. another name for the middle latitudes
3. another name for the high latitudes	7. term for the area between the Tropic of Cancer and the Tropic of Capricorn
4. where the sun stays overhead or nearly overhead all year long	

Core Concepts 3.3: Word Wise

Word Bank Choose one word from the word bank to fill in each blank. When you have finished, you will have a short summary of important ideas from the section.

Word Bank

evaporation   water cycle

Water, in one form or another, is constantly moving from Earth's

surface into the atmosphere and back to the surface. This process is called

the _____ and consists of four stages. The first stage is

_____, when water from a puddle, river, or sea changes

into water vapor. Then it rises into the sky. The vapor condenses into clouds

high in the atmosphere. The vapor eventually cools, forms droplets or

snowflakes, and falls to the ground as rain or snow. The precipitation is then

absorbed by the ground or a body of water, where it will start the water

cycle all over again.

Name _____   Class _____   Date _____

Core Concepts 3.4: Word Wise

Words In Context For each question below, write an answer that shows your
understanding of the boldfaced key term.

① How might people prepare for a **tropical cyclone**?

_____

_____

_____

② Why do people fear **tornadoes**?

_____

_____

_____

③ What is one reason that precipitation is so heavy in the **intertropical
convergence zone**?

_____

_____

_____

④ What weather conditions would you expect to see if a **hurricane** struck
your region?

_____

_____

_____

Core Concepts 3.5: Word Wise

Word Bank Choose one word from the word bank to fill in each blank. When you have finished, you will have a short summary of important ideas from the section.

Word Bank

tropical wet	tropical wet and dry
semiarid	arid
maritime	humid subtropical
subarctic	tundra

Earth has many climate types. Each one has a unique set of temperature ranges, kinds of precipitation, and prevailing winds. Areas near the Equator have a _____ climate, which is a type of climate much wetter than the _____ climate. The desert _____ climate is found in places where there it is generally hot with little precipitation. The _____ climate has wet summers and dry winters affected by the movement of the sun and shifting bands of rain over the Equator.

In cold, dry areas in far northern North America and Asia, the _____ climate is characterized by cool summers and bitterly cold, dry winters. _____ climates also have cool summers and very cold winters but have more precipitation, which allows pine trees to grow.

In areas where moist winds bring precipitation from the ocean, the climate is described as _____. In these areas, winters are mild and summers are hot. This is different from the _____ climate, which also exists where winds are moist. However, this type of climate has cool summers.

Name _____ Class _____ Date _____

Core Concepts 3.6: Word Wise

Vocabulary Quiz Show Some quiz shows ask a question and expect the contestant to give the answer. In other shows, the contestant is given an answer and must supply the question. If the blank is in the question column, write the question that would result in the answer given. If the question is supplied, write the appropriate answer.

QUESTION	ANSWER
① What do you call a grassland found in a tropical area with dry spells?	① _____
② _____	② deciduous trees
③ What is an interdependent community formed by plants and animals sharing an environment?	③ _____
④ _____	④ coniferous trees

Sum It Up

Make Connections Use the text and maps from this section to fill in the circles of this concept web. Describe the features of a tropical wet and dry climate.

1. Temperature

2. Latitudes and hemispheres

3. Precipitation

4. Air patterns

5. Connected ecosystems

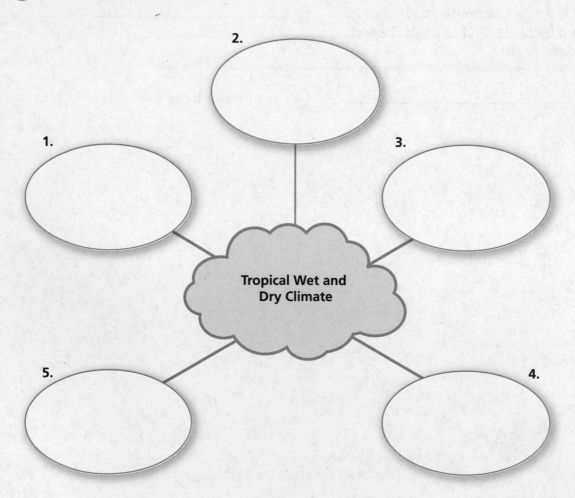

Tropical Wet and Dry Climate

1.

2.

3.

4.

5.

Core Concepts 4.1: Word Wise

Words In Context For each question below, write an answer that shows your understanding of the boldfaced key term.

(1) Why are trees considered a **renewable resource**?

_____

_____

(2) What makes water an important **natural resource**?

_____

_____

(3) Where do **fossil fuels** get their name?

_____

_____

(4) Name three factors that the **nonrenewable resources** of coal and petroleum have in common.

_____

_____

Core Concepts 4.2: Word Wise

Word Map Follow the model below to make a word map. The key term *colonization* is in the center oval. Write the definition in your own words at the upper left. In the upper right, list Characteristics, which means words or phrases that relate to the term. At the lower left list Noncharacteristics, which means words and phrases that would not be associated with it. In the lower right, draw a picture of the key term or use it in a sentence.

Definition in your own words	Characteristics
When settlers move to a region, they change it by bringing with them living things (like horses) and ideas (like music and religion).	• people starting farms • people putting up buildings and roads • people introducing plants and animals in a new area
NonCharacteristics	**Picture or Sentence**
• wilderness • any place untouched by humans • plants and animals that are native to the area	When people move into an area, they bring their plants, animals, ideas, and culture with them. This changes the area forever.

(center oval: colonization)

Now use the word map below to explore the meaning of the word *industrialization.* You may use your student text, a dictionary, and/or a thesaurus to complete each of the four sections.

Definition in your own words	Characteristics
NonCharacteristics	**Picture or Sentence**

(center oval: industrialization)

Make a word map of your own on a separate piece of paper for the word *suburbs.*

Name _____ Class _____ Date _____

Core Concepts 4.3: Word Wise

Sentence Builder Complete the sentences using the information you learned in this section. Be sure to include terminal punctuation.

(1) **Deforestation** is the result of _____

_____

(2) Air **pollution** occurs when _____

_____

(3) In an area with **biodiversity,** you would expect _____

_____

(4) A child with asthma who lives in an area with smog may suffer from

spillover because _____

_____

Sum It Up

Make Connections Use what you learned in this section to answer these questions.

(1) Think about how land use has changed since the 1800s. How do you think the world's supply of nonrenewable resources has been affected by these changes?

_____

_____

_____

(2) Imagine that a forest is being cut down to make room for new homes, farms, and roads. If a change in biodiversity takes place, is that an example of a spillover? Explain.

_____

_____

_____

(3) How is using public transportation like buses and subways a way to conserve energy?

_____

_____

_____

(4) Do you think building new suburbs helps or hurts the environment? Support your answer with evidence from the text or your personal experience.

_____

_____

_____

Core Concepts 5.1: Word Wise

Vocabulary Quiz Show Some quiz shows ask a question and expect the contestant to give the answer. In other shows, the contestant is given an answer and must supply the question. If the blank is in the question column, write the question that would result in the answer given. If the question is supplied, write the appropriate answer.

QUESTION	ANSWER
(1) _____	(1) incentive
(2) What describes the value of what you decide to give up when you make an economic choice?	(2) _____
(3) _____	(3) economics
(4) What do you call the amount of goods or services available for use?	(4) _____
(5) _____	(5) consumers
(6) What word describes the degree of desire for a good or a service?	(6) _____
(7) _____	(7) producers
(8) What is the term for having a limited quantity of resources to meet unlimited wants?	(8) _____

Core Concepts 5.2: Word Wise

Crossword Puzzle The clues describe key terms from this section. Fill in the numbered *Across* boxes with the correct key terms. Then, do the same with the *Down* clues.

Across	Down
1. an organized way for goods and services to be exchanged	5. a decline in economic growth for six or more months in a row
2. the money earned by selling goods and services	6. a general increase in prices over time
3. the act of a company concentrating on just a few goods or services	
4. the money left after subtracting the costs of doing business	

Core Concepts 5.3: Word Wise

Words In Context For each question below, write an answer that shows your understanding of the boldfaced key term.

(1) What makes a person's way of life important in a **traditional economy**?

_____

_____

_____

(2) Who makes economic decisions in a **mixed economy** and why?

_____

_____

_____

(3) How do new businesses benefit from the freedom of a **market economy**?

_____

_____

_____

(4) How does a **command economy** differ from a market economy?

_____

_____

_____

Copyright © Pearson Education, Inc., or its affiliates. All Rights Reserved.

Core Concepts 5.4: Word Wise

Word Map Follow the model below to make a word map. The key term *developed country* is in the center oval. Write the definition in your own words at the upper left. In the upper right, list Characteristics, which means words or phrases that relate to the term. At the lower left list Noncharacteristics, which means words and phrases that would not be associated with it. In the lower right, draw a picture of the key term or use it in a sentence.

Definition in your own words	Characteristics
a nation with a strong economy and a high standard of living such as Japan	• United States, Japan, Australia, many European nations • people have access to a lot of goods and services • people have medical care, homes, and wages

developed country

Noncharacteristics	Picture or Sentence
• developing country—a nation with a less productive economy and low standard of living such as Haiti • people struggle to have the basic necessities of life (food, clean water, shelter, and medical care)	Developed countries' strong economies are responsible for the high standard of living their people. Developing countries want to create strong economies for this reason.

Now use the word map below to explore the meaning of the word *technology*. You may use your student text, a dictionary, and/or a thesaurus to complete each of the four sections.

Definition in your own words	Characteristics

technology

Noncharacteristics	Picture or Sentence

Make word maps of your own on a separate piece of paper for these words: *development, gross domestic product,* and *productivity.*

Name _____ Class _____ Date _____

Core Concepts 5.5: Word Wise

Sentence Builder Complete the sentences using the information you learned in this section. Include terminal punctuation.

(1) Grain is one example of an **export** from the United States because it is

_____

(2) You might **trade** your _____ for _____

_____

(3) Consumers benefit from **free trade** because _____

_____

(4) China **imports** _____ from _____

_____

(5) An example of a **tariff** is a _____

_____

(6) The purpose of a **trade barrier** is _____

_____

Core Concepts 5.6: Word Wise

Word Bank Choose one word from the word bank to fill in each blank. When you have finished, you will have a short summary of important ideas from the section.

Word Bank

budget	credit
interest	invest
stocks	bonds
saving	

You have options for using your money wisely. For example,

_____ funds in a bank, credit union, or other financial

institution ensures that you will have money for future use. You can take

some of that money and _____ it. Hopefully this will earn

you a profit. One way to do this is to buy _____, which are

certificates from a business or the government promising to pay back your

money plus additional money. Another way to do it is to purchase

_____, which give you shares of ownership in a company.

Of course, people also buy expensive things such as a car or a home

even though they do not have enough money to pay for it in full. To do this,

most people use _____. This means that they agree to pay

for their purchase over time. As they pay back the loan, they will also have

to pay _____. If this seems complex, don't worry. You can

create and stick to a money-management plan called a(n)

_____. It will help you to save more and to avoid borrowing

too much money.

Name _____ Class _____ Date _____

Sum It Up

Think About It Use what you learned in this section to answer these questions about Myra and the way she uses her money.

(1) Your friend Myra is given $100. She wants to invest half of it so she can earn some more money. What do you think is the best way for her to do this? Why?

_____

_____

_____

(2) Myra plans to use the other $50 to buy a new pair of headphones. How might competition and specialization among headphone producers affect her choice?

_____

_____

_____

(3) Assume that Myra lives in a command economy. How do you think her headphone choices might be different from those in a market economy?

_____

_____

_____

(4) Now assume that Myra lives in a developing country. How might the supply and demand for $50 headphones be different than in a developed country?

_____

_____

_____

Core Concepts 6.1: Word Wise

Word Bank Choose one word from the word bank to fill in each blank. When you have finished, you will have a short summary of important ideas from the section.

Word Bank

demographers   birth rate

infant mortality rate   death rate

There are many ways to investigate and measure an area's population

growth. For example, a country's _____, or the number of

live births per 1,000 people in a year, is an important measurement.

_____, the scientists who study human populations, often

compare this number to the _____, which is the number of

deaths per 1,000 people in a year.

When the birth rate is higher than the death rate, the population is

growing. But when the death rate is higher than the birth rate, the

population does not grow. Such slowdowns in population often take place

when people do not have enough food and clean water. A lack of food and

clean water often leads to a higher _____, which is the

number of infant deaths per 1,000 births.

Name _____ Class _____ Date _____

Core Concepts 6.2: Word Wise

Words In Context For each question below, write an answer that shows your understanding of the boldfaced key term.

(1) Think of what a typical U.S. town or city is like on a busy Saturday afternoon, when many people are running errands, shopping, and participating in other activities. Which parts of a town do you think have the highest and lowest **population density** on a typical Saturday?

_____

_____

_____

_____

(2) How do you think changes in transportation over the past 100 years have changed **population distribution**?

_____

_____

_____

_____

Core Concepts 6.3: Word Wise

Word Map Follow the model below to make a word map. The key term *migration* is in the center oval. Write the definition in your own words at the upper left. In the upper right, list Characteristics, which means words or phrases that relate to the term. At the lower left list Noncharacteristics, which means words and phrases that would not be associated with it. In the lower right, draw a picture of the key term or use it in a sentence.

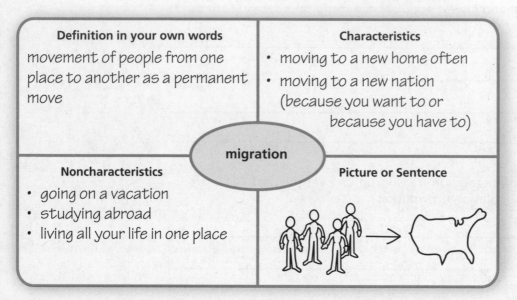

Definition in your own words

movement of people from one place to another as a permanent move

Characteristics

- moving to a new home often
- moving to a new nation (because you want to or because you have to)

migration

Noncharacteristics

- going on a vacation
- studying abroad
- living all your life in one place

Picture or Sentence

Now use the word map below to explore the meaning of the key term *push factor*. You may use your student text, a dictionary, and/or a thesaurus to complete each of the four sections.

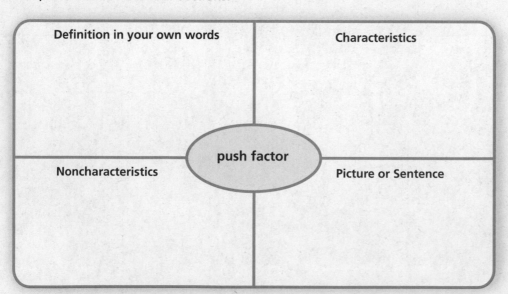

Definition in your own words

Characteristics

push factor

Noncharacteristics

Picture or Sentence

Make word maps of your own on a separate piece of paper for the following words: *emigrate, immigrate,* and *pull factor.*

Core Concepts 6.4: Word Wise

Vocabulary Quiz Show Some quiz shows ask a question and expect the contestant to give the answer. In other shows, the contestant is given an answer and must supply the question. If the blank is in the question column, write the question that would result in the answer given. If the question is supplied, write the appropriate answer.

QUESTION	ANSWER
① What do you call a poor, overcrowded urban area?	① _____
② _____	② urbanization
③ What occurs when the population of a city begins to spread away from the center of the city?	③ _____
④ _____	④ rural
⑤ A city is what type of area?	⑤ _____

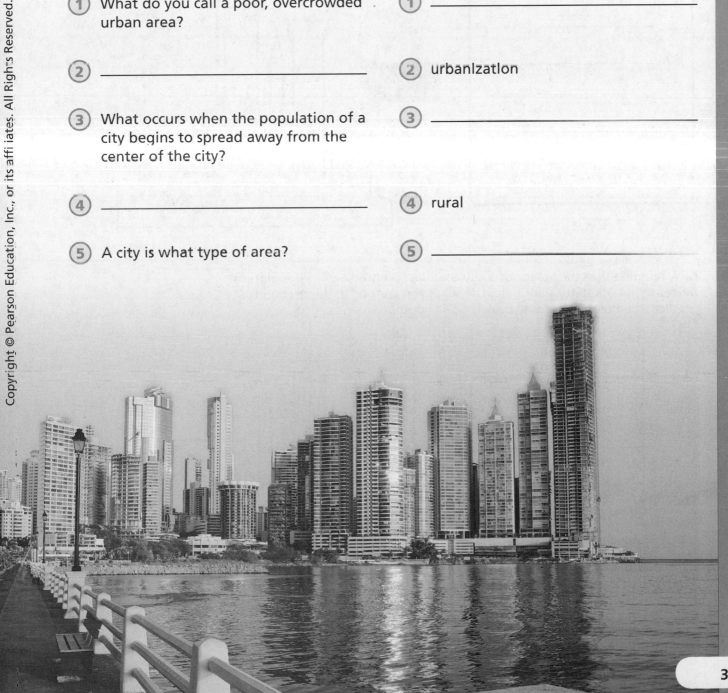

Sum It Up

Predict Imagine that you are a demographer. The mayor of a city that has recently experienced rapid population growth has asked you to investigate why his region is growing so quickly. Use what you learned in this section to predict three reasons for any city's growth.

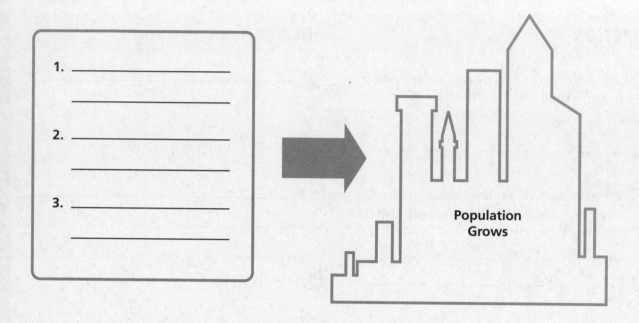

1. _____
   _____
2. _____
   _____
3. _____
   _____

Population Grows

Now imagine that the mayor of a city that has recently seen its population decrease has asked for your help. Use what you learned in this section to predict three reasons for any city's drop in population.

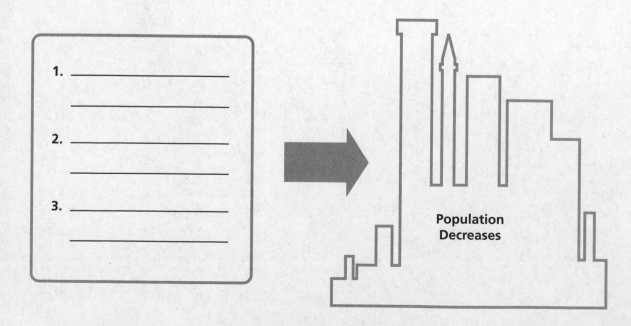

1. _____
   _____
2. _____
   _____
3. _____
   _____

Population Decreases

Core Concepts 7.1: Word Wise

Sentence Builder Complete the sentences using the information you learned in this section. Include terminal punctuation.

1 In modern American culture, one example of a **norm** is _____

_____

2 Examples of **cultural traits** are language, _____

_____

3 Human activities define the **cultural landscape** by _____

_____

4 A nation's **culture** includes its _____

_____

5 A **culture region** can extend beyond a nation's borders because _____

_____

Core Concepts 7.2: Word Wise

Vocabulary Quiz Show Some quiz shows ask a question and expect the contestant to give the answer. In other shows, the contestant is given an answer and must supply the question. If the blank is in the question column, write the question that would result in the answer given. If the question is supplied, write the appropriate answer.

QUESTION

① What is the basic unit of any society?

② _____

③ What word describes a human group that meets its basic needs in a shared culture?

④ _____

⑤ What term describes people who share the same standard of living based on their economic status?

⑥ _____

ANSWER

① _____

② nuclear family

③ _____

④ extended family

⑤ _____

⑥ social structure

Name _____ Class _____ Date _____

Core Concepts 7.3: Word Wise

Word Map Follow the model below to make a word map. The key term *communicate* is in the center oval. Write the definition in your own words at the upper left. In the upper right, list characteristics, which means words or phrases that relate to the term. At the lower left list noncharacteristics, which means words and phrases that would not be associated with it. In the lower right, draw a picture of the key term or use it in a sentence.

Definition in your own words	Characteristics
When you communicate, you pass along information that someone else can understand.	• convey information • spread news • understand others

communicate

Noncharacteristics	Picture or Sentence
• withhold information • conceal facts • not understand what others are saying • not knowing the language of an area • saying things that confuse others	 Do you have the books? Yes

Now use the word map below to explore the meaning of the word *language*. You may use your student text, a dictionary, and/or a thesaurus to complete each of the four sections.

Definition in your own words	Characteristics

language

Noncharacteristics	Picture or Sentence

Core Concepts 7.4: Word Wise

Words In Context For each question below, write an answer that shows your understanding of the boldfaced key term.

(1) Why do many people value **religion**, and what do they hope to gain from it?

_____

_____

_____

(2) Which situation would test your **ethics**: learning how to drive a car or deciding whether or not to copy someone else's homework? Explain.

_____

_____

_____

Name _____ Class _____ Date _____

Core Concepts 7.5: Word Wise

Crossword Puzzle The clues describe key terms from this section. Fill in the numbered *Across* boxes with the correct key terms. Then, do the same with the *Down* clues.

Across	Down
1. an art form that uses sound	4. written works of art
2. an idea reflected in artwork that relates to the whole world	5. a person who designs buildings
3. the process of designing and constructing buildings	6. works of art that are seen instead of read or heard

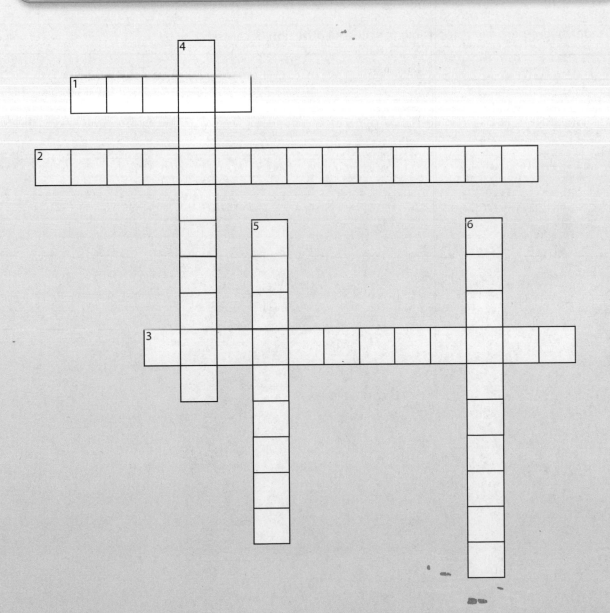

Core Concepts 7.6: Word Wise

Sentence Builder Complete the sentences using the information you learned in this section. Include terminal punctuation.

① Ideas such as _____ and _____ spread

outward from a **cultural hearth** when _____

_____

② One example of **diversity** is _____

_____

③ Traders were partially responsible for **cultural diffusion** because _____

_____

Name _____ Class _____ Date _____

Core Concepts 7.7: Word Wise

Word Bank Choose one word from the word bank to fill in each blank.
When you have finished, you will have a short summary of important ideas
from the section.

Word Bank

irrigate   science
technologies   standard of living

Throughout history, cultural development follows people's discoveries

about the natural world. New understandings in _____

helped ancient groups change from a life of hunting and gathering to

farming. For example, new _____ such as metalworking let

people create tools that helped them to clear land and to grow crops. When

people learned to _____ land, it increased the chances for

successful agriculture by making more land arable and providing some

protection against droughts.

As agriculture—and later industry—became central to world

economies, people were able to improve their _____ and

afford more goods and services.

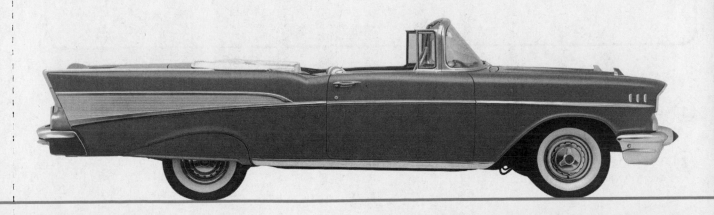

Sum It Up

Draw and Label Imagine that you have been given the chance to create a new town with new cultural elements. Draw a scene of everyday life in your new town, representing and labeling all of the concepts listed in the key.

KEY

A = cultural trait   **B** = language   **C** = art   **D** = technology

Answer these questions about your town on a separate piece of paper:

1 Describe the technology you included. How does it affect daily life in the town?

2 Describe diversity in the town. How does this diversity influence the town's overall culture?

Name _____ Class _____ Date _____

Core Concepts 8.1: Word Wise

Sentence Builder Complete the sentences using the information you learned in this section. Include terminal punctuation.

1 Two goals of a **government** are _____

_____

2 A **constitution** is a system _____

_____

3 In a **limited government**, _____

_____

4 In an **unlimited government**, _____

_____

5 **Tyranny** can result in an abuse of power such as _____

_____

Core Concepts 8.2: Word Wise

Crossword Puzzle The clues describe key terms from this section. Fill in the numbered *Across* boxes with the correct key terms. Then, do the same with the *Down* clues.

Across	Down
1. In the political system called _____, the government owns all the property.	5. another name for a nation or country
2. One person or a small group holds all the power in a(n) _____ government.	6. A(n) _____ consists of several nations or territories and may be quite large.
3. In a(n) _____, the citizens have political power.	7. a country led by a king or a queen
4. A city and surrounding area that form an independent state is a(n) _____.	

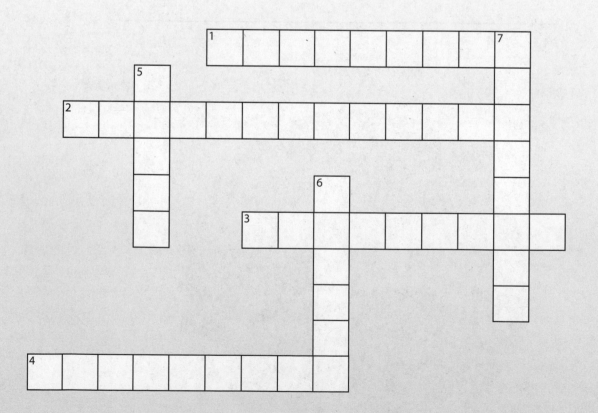

Name _____ Class _____ Date _____

Core Concepts 8.3: Word Wise

Word Map Follow the model below to make a word map. The term *unitary system* is in the center oval. Write the definition in your own words at the upper left. In the upper right, list Characteristics, which means words or phrases that relate to the term. At the lower left list Noncharacteristics, which means words and phrases that would not be associated with it. In the lower right, draw a picture of the key term or use it in a sentence.

Definition in your own words	Characteristics
a central government that makes laws for the whole country	• single government • centralized government • most nations today

unitary system

Noncharacteristics	Picture or Sentence
• federal system • divided government • confederal system • United States	A country with a unitary system has a very powerful central government.

Now use the word map below to explore the meaning of the term *federal system*. You may use your student text, a dictionary, and/or a thesaurus to complete each of the four sections.

Definition in your own words	Characteristics

federal system

Noncharacteristics	Picture or Sentence

Core Concepts 8.4: Word Wise

Words In Context For each question below, write an answer that shows your understanding of the boldfaced key term.

(1) How is a **treaty** an example of international cooperation?

_____

_____

_____

(2) How does **foreign policy** affect both the country that makes it and other countries?

_____

_____

_____

(3) How might a nation's foreign policy protect its **sovereignty**?

_____

_____

_____

(4) How are an American president's visits to foreign nations important for **diplomacy**?

_____

_____

_____

Name _____ Class _____ Date _____

Core Concepts 8.5: Word Wise

Word Bank Choose one word from the word bank to fill in each blank. When you have finished, you will have a short summary of important ideas from the section.

Word Bank

political party   civic life
citizens   civic participation
interest group

People born in the United States or who have completed the

naturalization process are U.S. _____. There are a number

of ways to take advantage of the privileges of citizenship. For example, you

may register to become a member of a _____ that reflects

your political views. Becoming involved with this group and other

organizations is a simple, effective way of participating in

_____. Voting, speaking out in meetings, signing petitions,

or simply staying informed are other kinds of _____.

If there is a certain issue about which you feel strongly, you may want to

join a related _____ dedicated to that particular cause.

49

Sum It Up

Predict Read each boldfaced statement. Think about what you read in this section. Then, consider the change given in the sentence starters. In each case you are making a logical prediction based on what you learned in this chapter. Include terminal punctuation.

1. **Country A is a representative democracy with a federal system of government.**

   If Country A switches to a unitary system of government, then _____

   _____

   _____

2. **Country B is made up of territory on one continent.**

   If Country B changes its foreign policy to become an overseas empire, then

   _____

   _____

3. **Country C has had the same constitution for 150 years.**

   If Country C's government becomes authoritarian, then _____

   _____

   _____

4. **Country D has a limited government made up of people from several political parties.**

   If Country D changes to unlimited government, then _____

   _____

   _____

5. **Country E has always encouraged the civic participation of its citizens.**

   If Country E's government becomes a tyranny, then _____

   _____

   _____

Core Concepts 9.1: Word Wise

Crossword Puzzle The clues are definitions of key terms from this section. Fill in the numbered *Across* boxes with the correct key terms. Then, do the same with the *Down* clues.

Across	Down
1. a length of time that is important because of certain events or developments that occurred during that era	3. a person who studies, describes, and explains the past
2. a graphic organizer that shows events in the chronological order in which they happened	4. a list of events in the order in which they took place
	5. the time before humans invented writing

Core Concepts 9.2: Word Wise

Words In Context For each question below, write an answer that shows your understanding of the boldfaced key term.

(1) Why is an article written about a famous explorer considered a **secondary source**?

_____

_____

_____

(2) Why do museums collect and display **artifacts**?

_____

_____

_____

(3) When researching a topic, why must you be on guard against **bias**?

_____

_____

_____

(4) If you were doing a project about a famous battle, what **primary sources** might you use?

_____

_____

_____

Name _____ Class _____ Date _____

Core Concepts 9.3: Word Wise

Word Bank Choose one word from the word bank to fill in each blank. When you have finished, you will have a short summary of important ideas from the section.

Word Bank
archaeology
anthropology
oral tradition

For centuries before people began to record information by writing,

history and culture was communicated to younger generations through

_____. By passing down information through songs and

storytelling, people were able to continue their traditions for hundreds

of years

Today, people involved in the field of _____ study this

practice as well as other aspects of how different cultures developed. These

historians also depend on the findings of the people who work in

_____. Using evidence from artifacts, scientists in this field

determine how people behaved and what their culture was like.

Core Concepts 9.4: Word Wise

Word Map Follow the model below to make a word map. The key term *locate* is in the center oval. Write the definition in your own words at the upper left. In the upper right, list Characteristics, which means words or phrases that relate to the term. At the lower left list Noncharacteristics, which means words and phrases that would not be associated with it. In the lower right, draw a picture of the key term or use it in a sentence.

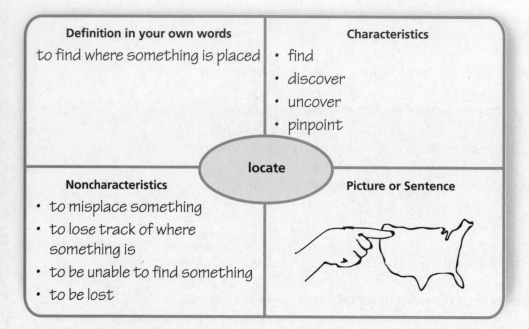

Definition in your own words
to find where something is placed

Characteristics
- find
- discover
- uncover
- pinpoint

locate

Noncharacteristics
- to misplace something
- to lose track of where something is
- to be unable to find something
- to be lost

Picture or Sentence

Now use the word map below to explore the meaning of the word *historical map*. You may use your student text, a dictionary, and/or a thesaurus to complete each of the four sections.

Definition in your own words

Characteristics

historical map

Noncharacteristics

Picture or Sentence

Name _____ Class _____ Date _____

Sum It Up

Be a History Detective Imagine that it has just been revealed that a famous American was actually a spy for another country. You are a historian collecting information for a documentary about this American's secret life. Explain how you would use each type of resource listed in the table's column headings. Include a specific example of each kind of resource. (You will need to use your imagination for this part.)

Primary Sources	Secondary Sources	Artifacts

Essential Question

How can you measure success?

Preview Before you begin this chapter, think about the Essential Question. Understanding how the Essential Question connects to your life will help you understand the chapter you are about to read.

Connect to Your Life

1 Think of some ways to measure success in the categories shown in the table below. List at least one way in each column. For example, under family you could list getting along with your siblings.

Measures of Personal Success			
Family	Friends	School	Other (Sports, Hobbies, Chores)

2 Look at the table. Compare the ways to measure success. How are they alike? How do they differ?

_____

_____

_____

Connect to the Chapter

3 Think about how to measure a country's success. For instance, a strong economy shows economic success. Preview the chapter's headings, photos, and graphics. In the table below, list one way to measure success in each category, and predict if the United States has achieved success in each. Include a reason: for example, if you think that the United States has too many social services that result in high taxes, it would show a lack of success.

Measures of National Success			
Economy	Politics	Social Services	Environment

4 Read the chapter. Then, circle your correct predictions.

Name _____ Class _____ Date _____

Connect to myStory: Finding Opportunity

① Are you a "new American" who just recently arrived? Were you born in the United States? Were your parents? Do you know of any immigrants in your background?

_____

_____

_____

② Have you ever visited another country? What things did you see there that were different from the United States? If you have never visited another country, write at least two things you would expect to be different in another nation.

_____

_____

_____

③ Suppose you were Vy's parents coming to live in a new country. What things would you be most worried about?

_____

_____

_____

④ What does Vy's life tell you about the opportunities immigrants have found in the United States?

_____

_____

Word Wise

Words In Context For each question below, write an answer that shows your understanding of the boldfaced key term.

(1) When thousands of Europeans left their homes in the 1800s and 1900s, how did this effect **migration** to the United States?

_____

_____

_____

(2) Why is the **climate** for most of the continental United States considered **temperate**?

_____

_____

_____

(3) Where is **population density** at its lowest and its highest within the United States?

_____

_____

_____

(4) What is a **metropolitan area** like?

_____

_____

_____

Name _____ Class _____ Date _____

Take Notes

Map Skills Use the maps in your book to make a key and to label the Places to Know on the outline map below.

Places to Know!

Physical Features	Cities
Rocky Mountains	Washington, D.C.
Great Plains	Los Angeles
Atlantic Ocean	New York
Pacific Ocean	Chicago

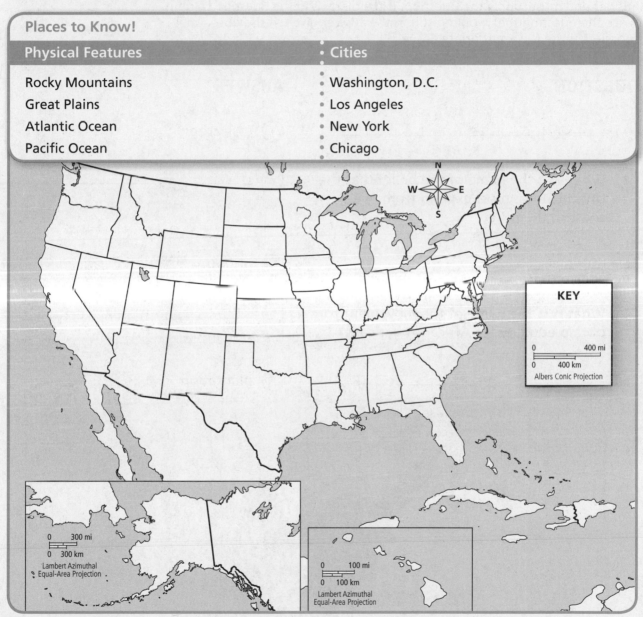

KEY

0 — 400 mi
0 — 400 km
Albers Conic Projection

0 — 300 mi
0 — 300 km
Lambert Azimuthal
Equal-Area Projection

0 — 100 mi
0 — 100 km
Lambert Azimuthal
Equal-Area Projection

Essential Question

How have natural resources created financial wealth for the United States?

_____

_____

_____

Word Wise

Vocabulary Quiz Show Some quiz shows ask a question and expect the contestant to give the answer. In other shows, the contestant is given an answer and must supply the question. If the blank is in the question column, write the question that would result in the answer given. If the question is supplied, write the appropriate answer.

QUESTION

(1) _____

(2) What was the name of the belief that the United States must expand from one coast to the other?

(3) _____

(4) What was the name of the movement to obtain equality for African Americans?

(5) _____

ANSWER

(1) cash crop

(2) _____

(3) dissenter

(4) _____

(5) plantation

Name _____ Class _____ Date _____

Take Notes

Sequence In this section you read about the history of the United States. Complete the timeline below by writing the name of the event that occurred for each date or time period indicated.

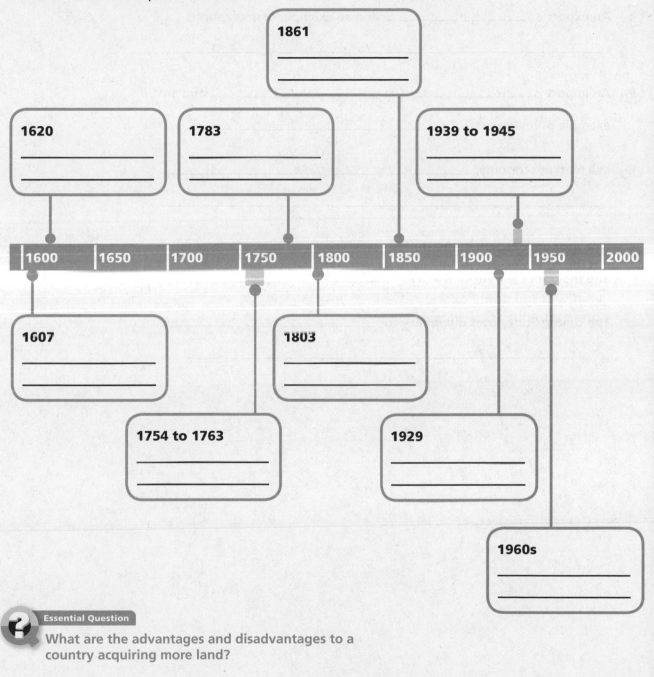

1861
_____
_____

1620
_____
_____

1783
_____
_____

1939 to 1945
_____
_____

| 1600 | 1650 | 1700 | 1750 | 1800 | 1850 | 1900 | 1950 | 2000 |

1607
_____
_____

1803
_____
_____

1754 to 1763
_____
_____

1929
_____
_____

1960s
_____
_____

Essential Question

What are the advantages and disadvantages to a country acquiring more land?

_____

_____

_____

Word Wise

Sentence Builder Complete the sentences using the information you learned in this section. Include terminal punctuation.

(1) An **export** is _____, and an example of an **export** is

_____

(2) An **import** is _____, and an

example of an **import** is _____

(3) In a **market economy,** _____

_____

(4) One **economic region** in the United States is _____,

and the goods produced there are _____

(5) The United States uses **diplomacy** to _____

_____

Name _____ Class _____ Date _____

Take Notes

Cause and Effect Use what you have learned about immigration to the United States to complete the graphic organizer below. Write one effect of immigration in each of the three categories.

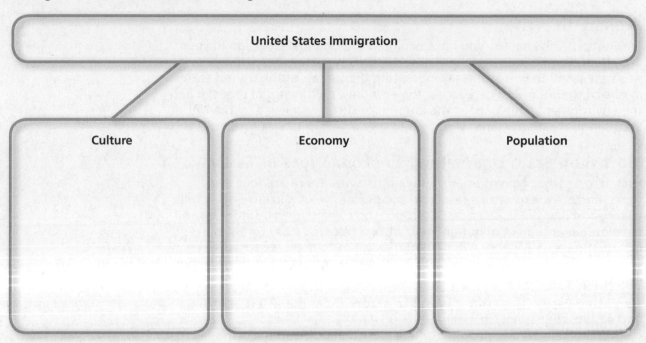

United States Immigration

Culture

Economy

Population

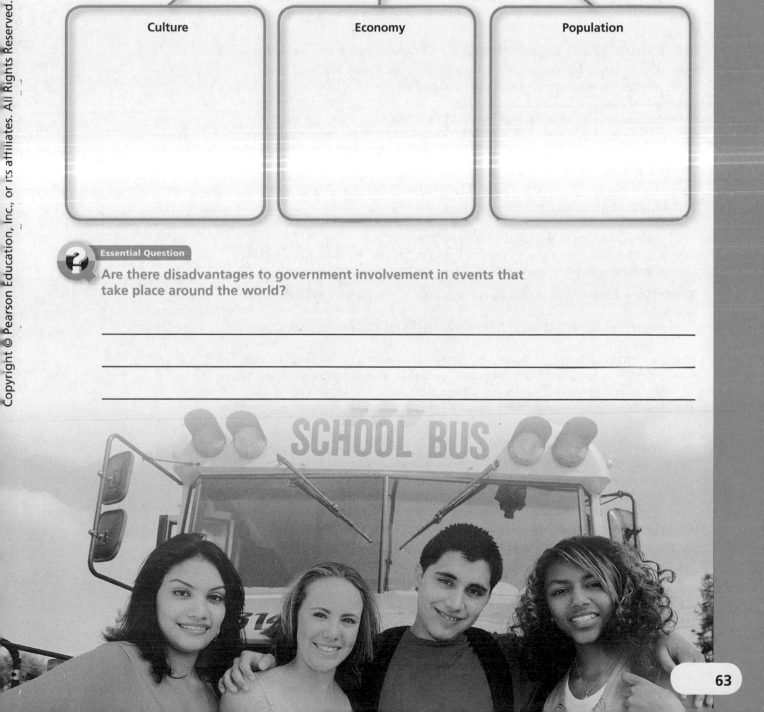

Essential Question

Are there disadvantages to government involvement in events that take place around the world?

_____

_____

_____

Essential Question **Writer's Workshop**

How can you measure success?

Prepare to Write

Throughout this chapter, you have explored the Essential Question in your text, journal, and On Assignment at myWorldGeography.com. Use what you've learned to write an essay measuring the success of the United States in one of the following categories: the economy, politics, social services, and the environment. Think about the amount of success achieved by the United States in that category and what caused the success or lack of success.

Workshop Skill: Understand the Four Types of Essays

First, decide what type of essay you want to write. There are four essay types: narrative, expository, research, and persuasive. A narrative essay tells a story and has a plot, characters, setting, and climax. An expository essay develops an argument about an idea, while a research essay contains information and evidence from a broad range of sources. A persuasive essay tries to get the reader to agree with a position by presenting evidence that supports the position.

Narrative Essay This essay is most like a story. It has characters, a setting, and a plot.

- Characters are the people that the story is about, and the setting is the time and place in which the story happens.
- A plot is the sequence of events that take place. Plots include conflict and lead up to a climax, which is the turning point of the story.

Expository Essay This essay has a main idea supported by evidence and examples.

- An introductory paragraph opens with a thesis sentence that states the main idea.
- The introduction is followed by body paragraphs. Each one discusses a point that supports the main idea. Evidence and examples are used to show that the supporting points are true.
- The conclusion sums up the essay by restating the thesis and supporting points.

Research Essay This essay has the same structure as an expository essay. The difference lies in the type of evidence used to prove supporting points.

- Evidence and examples should come from a broad range of reliable sources.
- Writers use quotations, footnotes, and a bibliography to show where they located evidence.

Persuasive Essay This essay is written when the author wants to convince readers to adopt an opinion or take action.

- The introduction tells why the topic is important. Then the thesis statement explains what the writer wants readers to think or do.
- In the body paragraphs, the writer uses strong arguments and evidence to prove the supporting points.
- The conclusion reviews the main points and urges the reader to adopt the opinion or take the action mentioned.

Identify Essay Types

Read the descriptions in the table below. In the column on the right, identify the essay described as narrative, expository, research, or persuasive.

Essay Description	Type
1. The essay tells a story about a nation in which three ethnic groups continually clash due to religious differences. The story ends when two of these groups make a truce.	_____
2. The essay states that access to medical care helps a developing nation's economy succeed by offering a more stable, healthy workforce. The essay includes graphs, charts, statistics, and quotations. Sources are listed in endnotes.	_____
3. The essay discusses how an aging population creates difficulties for a nation and explains three general problems that occur when there are more retirees than current workers.	_____
4. The essay urges businesses and environmentalists to compromise about natural resource development so that both sides can benefit. It cites examples of nations in which some natural resources have been used with minimal damage to the environment.	_____

Plan Your Essay

Use the following questions to help you make some decisions about your essay.

1. What do I want to say about the success or lack of success in the United States?

_____

_____

2. Do I want to tell a story, to explain an idea, present evidence, or persuade others?

_____

_____

3. Which essay type will best help me to accomplish my goal? _____

Draft Your Essay

Outline your essay. You will need an introductory paragraph, three body paragraphs, and a conclusion. Use the outline to write your essay. Then, proofread carefully.

Name _____ Class _____ Date _____

Essential Question

Is conflict unavoidable?

Preview Before you begin this chapter, think about the Essential Question. Understanding how the Essential Question connects to your life will help you understand the chapter you are about to read.

Connect to Your Life

(1) What has caused conflicts in your family, school, community, or state? Name two recent conflicts.

_____

_____

(2) Listed in the table below are three reasons for conflicts. Rate how apt each one is to cause conflict, with 1 being likely and 5 being unlikely. To help decide, you may want to consider the conflicts you named.

Reason for Conflict	How likely is it to cause conflict?				
Misunderstandings	1	2	3	4	5
Power struggles	1	2	3	4	5
Differences	1	2	3	4	5
Other: _____	1	2	3	4	5

Connect to the Chapter

(3) Now think about sources of conflict in a country or region that can lead to tension (such as differences in economic opportunity). Preview the chapter by skimming its headings, photographs, and graphics. In the web below, predict sources of conflict.

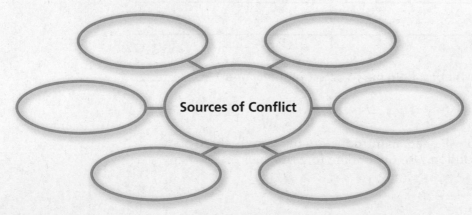

(4) After reading the chapter, return to this page and highlight your accurate predictions

Name _____ Class _____ Date _____

Connect to myStory: Drawing on Heritage

① In Alyssa's story, you read about some of the traditional foods she enjoys sharing with her co-workers. Name at least three dishes they had at their "Country Food" luncheon.

② Now, think about foods that you enjoy that come from your own heritage. Write the name of at least two dishes and describe what is in them.

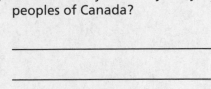

③ How do the traditional foods that Alyssa and you enjoy reflect the resources in the places where your ancestors lived?

_____
_____
_____

④ What does Alyssa's story tell you about the aboriginal peoples of Canada?

_____
_____
_____

Name _____ Class _____ Date _____

Word Wise

Crossword Puzzle The clues describe key terms from this section. Fill in the numbered *Across* boxes with the correct key terms. Then, do the same with the *Down* clues.

Across	Down
1. a layer of soil that is frozen all year	4. any form of water, such as rain, snow, sleet, or hail, that falls from the sky to the ground
2. an ice mass formed from years of accumulated snow that may be moving very slowly	5. the area where warm and cold seawater combine
3. a treeless area lying above the tree line in an Arctic region that has permanently frozen subsoil	

Name _____ Class _____ Date _____

Take Notes

Map Skills Use the maps in your book to make a key and to label the Places to Know on the outline map below.

Places to Know!

Physical Features	Cities
Canadian Cordillera	Ottawa
Canadian Shield	Montreal
Arctic Archipelago	Toronto
St. Lawrence River Valley	Calgary

KEY

0 ————— 400 mi
0 ————— 400 km
Lambert Azimuthal
Equal-Area Projection

Essential Question

What agreements reflect cooperation between the United States and Canada? How do they do so?

_____

_____

_____

Name _____ Class _____ Date _____

Word Wise

Words In Context For each question below, write an answer that shows your understanding of the boldfaced key term.

(1) What was the **compromise** the British made in the Quebec Act?

_____

_____

_____

(2) Name two groups that are part of the **First Nations** and one group that is not.

_____

_____

_____

(3) Why was Canada originally called **New France,** and what happened to change its name?

_____

_____

_____

(4) Canada is a **dominion** of which nation?

_____

_____

_____

(5) How is a Canadian **province** similar to a state in the United States?

_____

_____

_____

Name _____ Class _____ Date _____

Take Notes

Sequence Use what you have read about Canada's history to complete this timeline. Identify the key event associated with each date on the timeline, then give a brief description of the event and its significance.

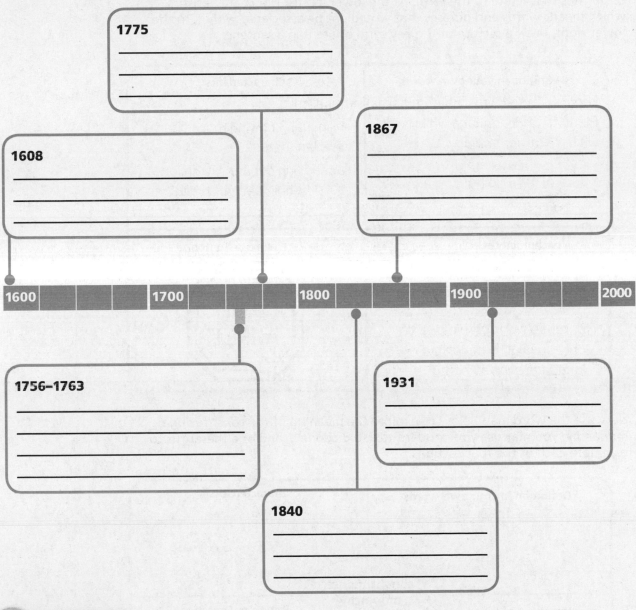

1775
_____
_____
_____

1608
_____
_____
_____

1867
_____
_____
_____

1600   1700   1800   1900   2000

1756–1763
_____
_____
_____
_____

1931
_____
_____
_____

1840
_____
_____
_____

? Essential Question

How did Canada gain its independence from Britain?

_____

_____

_____

Word Wise

Word Map Follow the model below to make a word map. The key term *cultural mosaic* is in the center oval. Write the definition in your own words at the upper left. In the upper right, list Characteristics, which means words or phrases that relate to the term. At the lower left list Noncharacteristics, which means words and phrases that would not be associated with it. In the lower right, draw a picture of the key term or use it in a sentence.

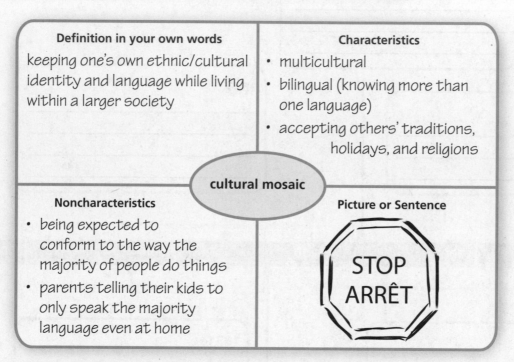

Definition in your own words
keeping one's own ethnic/cultural identity and language while living within a larger society

Characteristics
- multicultural
- bilingual (knowing more than one language)
- accepting others' traditions, holidays, and religions

cultural mosaic

Noncharacteristics
- being expected to conform to the way the majority of people do things
- parents telling their kids to only speak the majority language even at home

Picture or Sentence
STOP
ARRÊT

Now use the word map below to explore the meaning of the *constitutional monarchy*. You may use your student text, a dictionary, and/or a thesaurus to complete each of the four sections.

Definition in your own words

Characteristics

constitutional monarchy

Noncharacteristics

Picture or Sentence

Make a word map of your own on a separate piece of paper for the term *plural society*.

Name _____   Class _____   Date _____

Take Notes

Compare and Contrast Use the Venn diagram below to compare and contrast Canada and the United States. Include each nation's past and present relationship with Great Britain, the structure of their governments, their roles in the world, and how each nation has responded to racial diversity. For example, in the intersection where you write the elements that are the same, note that Canada and the United States both began as British colonies.

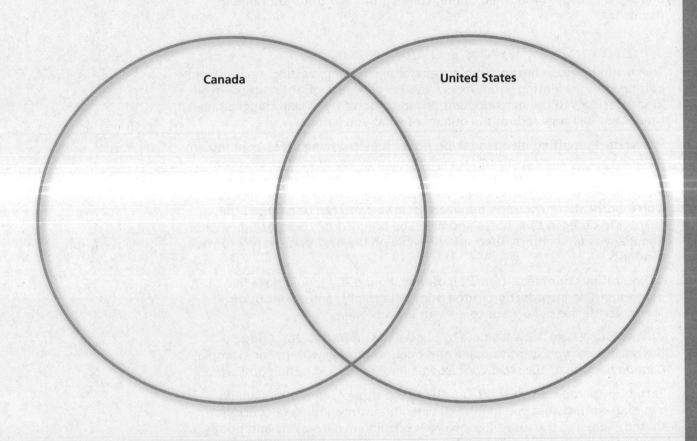

Canada   United States

Essential Question

Why is Canada known as a peacekeeping nation?

_____

_____

_____

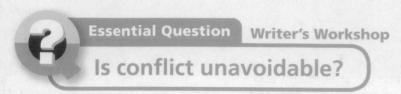

Essential Question **Writer's Workshop**

Is conflict unavoidable?

Prepare to Write

Throughout this chapter, you have explored the Essential Question in your text, journal, and On Assignment at myWorldGeography.com. Use what you've learned to write an essay describing how the country of Canada managed to avoid bloodshed during conflicts in three different times in its history.

Workshop Skill: Use the Writing Process

The writing process has four main steps: brainstorming, writing, revising and editing, and presenting your work. All writers go through these steps—from kindergartners to the most popular novelists. Don't try to skip steps to save time! That will only reduce the quality of what you write.

Prewrite Prewriting involves taking notes, brainstorming ideas, creating an outline, and gathering information that you may use in your essay. When you read the chapter and completed the journal pages, you took notes. When brainstorming, write down all your thoughts as they occur to you. Don't worry about choosing between them yet. You can also reread the chapter in order to take notes and help you brainstorm. Look for times when Canada avoided conflict. Then use the table on the next page to record your thoughts.

As you refine your ideas, create an outline. Your essay should have five paragraphs: an introduction, three body paragraphs, and a conclusion. Jot down the facts you want to present in each one.

Write Your Essay Now it's time to put your ideas into words. Consider the main point you want to make and open your essay with it. For example: *Canada has one of the most conflict-free histories of any nation on Earth.*

Each body paragraph must discuss one of the three examples of Canada avoiding conflict that you identified when brainstorming. Your conclusion should "sum up" the essay. Restate your opening in a new way and briefly identify your three examples again.

Revise and Edit Your Essay Most people spend a lot of time revising. Why? They reread their essay aloud to find out if the sentences "flow." They rewrite to make sentences concise and organize ideas better. They check for grammar and spelling mistakes, remove sentence fragments, and fix run-on sentences. All of these things can trip up your readers so that they don't understand your essay. Take your time with this step. It may help to read your essay aloud to another person. He or she will tell you if something is confusing or unclear. Listen to what the person says.

Present Your Essay Rewrite your essay on a clean sheet of paper. Double space and include your name, date, and an essay title. Remember, this is your polished, final version. You want it to look and read its best!

Try Brainstorming

First, you may want to reread Section 2 of the chapter to refresh your memory. Then, answer these questions in order to pull together your thoughts for the essay:

When did Canada face conflict?	How was the conflict handled? (fighting or negotiation)	Was this a good example of conflict avoidance? (using negotiation instead of force)	
		YES	NO
		YES	NO
		YES	NO
		YES	NO
		YES	NO

Now consider the rows in which you answered YES in the third column. You are going to select three of these to write about.

Draft Your Essay

Use the information you brainstormed above to write a your essay on another paper. You should have five paragraphs: an introduction, three body paragraphs, and a conclusion. Follow the steps in the writing process to revise, edit, and present your essay.

Name _____ Class _____ Date _____

How much does geography shape a country?

Preview Before you begin this chapter, think about the Essential Question. Understanding how the Essential Question connects to your life will help you understand the chapter you are about to read.

Connect to Your Life

① Think about how the geographic elements in the table below have affected your life. Complete the table below with your ideas.

Personal Influence of Geographic Elements				
Parks, Lakes, Rivers	Local Weather	Local Crops	School Size	Recreational Activities

② In what ways can these elements affect each other? For example, in what way can cold weather affect the type of recreational activities in a region?

_____

_____

Connect to the Chapter

③ Before you read the chapter, flip through every page and note the red headings, maps, and pictures. Think about ways that the influence of geography on families and communities applies to nations as well. In the table below, predict how geography has shaped Mexico.

Influences of Geographic Elements on a Country				
Physical Features	Climate	Natural Resources	Population	Culture

④ After reading the chapter, return to this page. Were your predictions accurate? Why or why not?

_____

_____

76

Connect to myStory: A Long Way From Home

1 Think about ways that your life is like Carolina's life. What challenges face your family every day? How does school play a role in your life? What are your hopes for the future?

_____

_____

2 Use this Venn diagram to compare your life with Carolina's life. Think about family challenges, school, and hopes for the future.

Your Life   **Both**   **Carolina's Life**

3 In this table, list the challenges Carolina faces as she tries to help her family meet its goals.

Daily Life	Making a Living	Getting an Education

4 How do you think these challenges are affecting the people of Mexico? Write your predictions below.

_____

_____

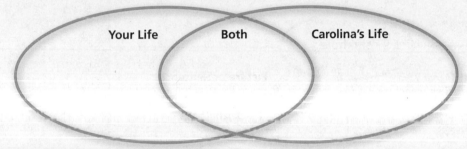

77

Word Wise

Word Map Follow the model below to make a word map. The key term *sinkhole* is in the center oval. Write the definition in your own words at the upper left. In the upper right, list Characteristics, which means words or phrases that relate to the term. At the lower left list Noncharacteristics, which means words and phrases that would not be associated with it. In the lower right, draw a picture of the key term or use it in a sentence.

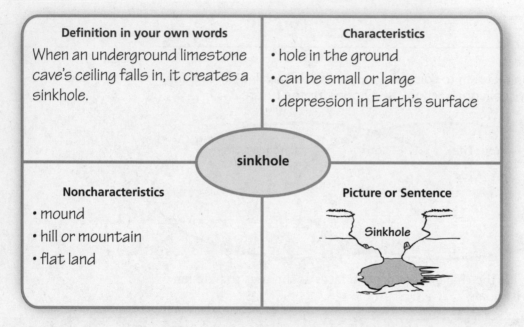

Definition in your own words

When an underground limestone cave's ceiling falls in, it creates a sinkhole.

Characteristics

• hole in the ground
• can be small or large
• depression in Earth's surface

sinkhole

Noncharacteristics

• mound
• hill or mountain
• flat land

Picture or Sentence

Sinkhole

Now use the word map below to explore the meaning of the word *altitude*. You may use your student text, a dictionary, and/or a thesaurus to complete each of the four sections.

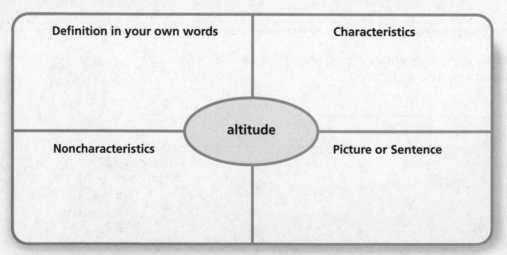

Definition in your own words

Characteristics

altitude

Noncharacteristics

Picture or Sentence

Make word maps of your own on a separate piece of paper for these key terms: *irrigate* and *hydroelectric power*.

Name _____ Class _____ Date _____

Take Notes

Map Skills Use the maps in your book to make a key and to label the Places to Know on the outline map below.

Places to Know!	
Physical Features	**Cities**
Sierra Madre Occidental	Merida
Mexican Plateau	Mexico City
Rio Grande	Guadalajara
Yucatán Peninsula	

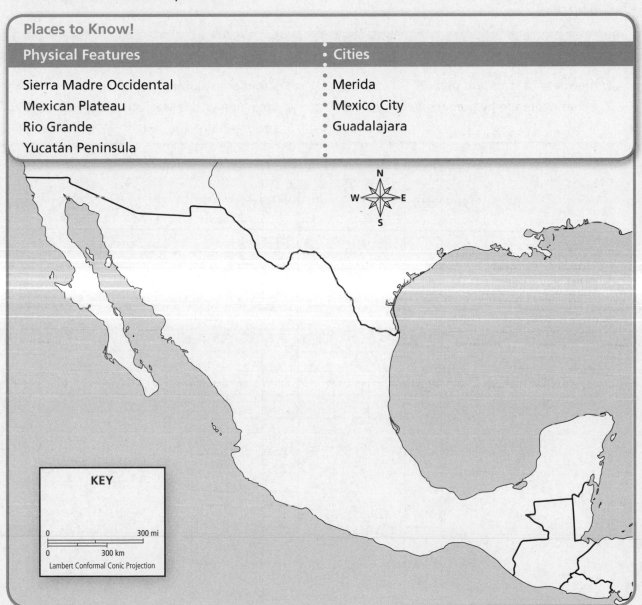

KEY

0 _____ 300 mi

0 _____ 300 km

Lambert Conformal Conic Projection

Essential Question

What is one reason Mexico's population growth has concentrated near Mexico City?

_____

_____

_____

Word Wise

Crossword Puzzle The clues describe key terms from this section. Fill in the numbered *Across* boxes with the correct key terms. Then, do the same with the *Down* clues.

Across	Down
1. the study of stars and planets	3. a soldier-explorer
2. a channel made by humans to carry water	4. the name of the Mexican war of 1910–1917
	5. another name for corn

Name _____ Class _____ Date _____

Take Notes

Cause and Effect Use what you have learned about the history of Mexico to complete the table below. The first row has been completed for you.

Mexican History	
Event	Result
During the 1400s, the Aztec empire flourished.	The Aztec language, religion, and army spread throughout Mexico.
Hernan Cortés defeated the Aztec.	
In the 1700s, Spain sent new rulers to Mexico.	
In 1810, the Mexicans revolted against their leadership.	
Porfirio Díaz led Mexico.	
In 1910, the Mexicans revolted against their leadership.	

Essential Question

How did Mexico's geography and the struggle for resources affect the history of Mexico?

_____

_____

_____

Word Wise

Words In Context For each question below, write an answer that shows your understanding of the boldfaced key term.

(1) Why did Mexican leaders adopt the **free market** economic system, and what happened to the Mexican economy when they did?

_____

_____

_____

(2) For how many years did the **Institutional Revolutionary Party (PRI)** control the Mexican government, and why were the people frustrated by it?

_____

_____

_____

(3) In what year did the **National Action Party (PAN)** first win the Mexican presidency, and what happened after that?

_____

_____

_____

(4) How do **remittances** help to support both Mexican families and the national economy?

_____

_____

_____

Name _____ Class _____ Date _____

Take Notes

Main Ideas and Details In this section, you read about the modern government, culture, and economy of Mexico. Each of the topics below corresponds to a heading in this section of the chapter. Use the graphic organizer below to record the main ideas and details about these topics.

Topic: Governing Mexico

Main idea:

Details:

Topic: People and Culture

Main idea:

Details:

Topic: Mexico's Economy

Main idea:

Details:

Topic: Trade

Main idea:

Details:

Essential Question

How has Mexico benefited from having abundant deposits of oil?

_____

_____

_____

Name _____ Class _____ Date _____

How much does geography shape a country?

Prepare to Write

Throughout this chapter, you have explored the Essential Question in your text, journal, and On Assignment at myWorldGeography.com. Use what you've learned to write an essay describing how geography has shaped Mexico. You may include the following: the economy, politics, natural resources, and environment of the nation. In each category, consider how geography helped or hindered Mexico.

Workshop Skill: Write Body Paragraphs

Consider the main point you want to make in your essay. Phrase it as a thesis statement in your first (introduction) paragraph. For example, *The geographic variety of Mexico has both helped and hindered the nation.* In your introduction, support your thesis with three ideas.

In this lesson, you will learn how to write the body paragraphs of your essay—the three paragraphs in the middle of a five-paragraph essay. Each body paragraph should develop one of the ideas you listed in the introduction that supports your thesis statement. Each body paragraph takes the idea further by giving details or evidence.

Write a Topic Sentence Start each paragraph with a topic sentence. A topic sentence must clearly state the main idea of the body paragraph, connect that idea to the essay's thesis, and provide a transition from the previous paragraph. In this case, that paragraph was the introduction.

Support the Topic Sentence With Details and Facts After your topic sentence, you must explain and support your point with discussion and details. Discussion sentences connect and explain your main point and supporting details. Details provide the actual facts that prove that what you say is true.

End With a Concluding Sentence Finish your paragraph with one to two sentences that reflects your topic sentence and draws the discussion and details together. In the example below, the concluding sentence explains why few people live to the north or south of the Mexican Plateau. The final sentence also relates back to the topic sentence.

Here is a sample body paragraph:

Topic sentence *Most of the population of Mexico lives on the Mexican Plateau, although there are several problems with this region.*

Supporting detail *The soil in this area is soft, and some structures built there have actually sunk over time.*

Supporting detail *Two mountain chains flank the Mexican Plateau. They prevent air pollution from crowded Mexico City from escaping into the atmosphere.*

Supporting discussion *As a result, Mexico City has some of the worst smog in the world.*

Supporting detail *Fault lines also run through the Mexican Plateau, causing dangerous earthquakes.*

Concluding sentence *However, since it is almost as dry as a desert to the north of the Mexican Plateau and there are thick rain forests to the south, it is not surprising that so many people live on the Plateau.*

Write a Body Paragraph

Now write your own body paragraph for your essay. You may not have four supporting details or discussion; three will be sufficient.

Topic sentence _____

_____

Supporting (detail/discussion) _____

_____

Supporting (detail/discussion) _____

_____

Supporting (detail/discussion) _____

_____

Supporting (detail/discussion) _____

_____

Concluding sentence _____

_____

Draft Your Essay

Use the body paragraph above in your complete essay. Write it on your own paper. Be sure that each of your body paragraphs has a topic sentence, supporting details, and a concluding sentence.

Name _____ Class _____ Date _____

Is it better to be independent or interdependent?

Preview Before you begin this chapter, think about the Essential Question. Understanding how the Essential Question connects to your life will help you understand the chapter you are about to read.

Connect to Your Life

(1) Think about ways in which you are independent and ways in which you rely upon others. For example, you may be independent in doing your homework, but you are interdependent on your parents for a home and food. In the chart below, list at least one advantage and one disadvantage of being independent and interdependent.

	Advantages	Disadvantages
Independent		
Interdependent		

(2) Think about situations in which you might prefer to be independent or interdependent. How do these situations differ?

_____

_____

Connect to the Chapter

(3) Before you read this chapter, flip through it. Look at the headings and pictures. In the Venn diagram below, predict ways in which the countries in Central America and the Caribbean are independent or interdependent.

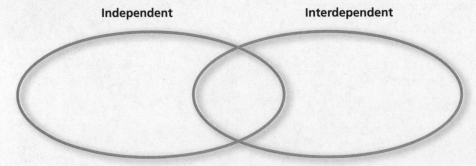

Independent   Interdependent

(4) After reading the chapter, return to this page. Circle your predictions that were correct.

Name _____ Class _____ Date _____

Connect to myStory: Working for the Future

1 On the table below, list ways in which Luís is independent and interdependent.

Luís's Personal Independence and Interdependence		
	• Independence	• Interdependence
Family		
Friends		
School		

2 Compare what you wrote about Luís to your own life on the Essential Question Preview page. On the table above, underline or highlight similiarities.

3 Based on your preview of the chapter and what you read about Luís's life, make the following predictions:

Do you think the standard of living is adequate for those who live in the region's rural areas? Explain.

_____

_____

_____

What type of work does Luís do? Can this part of the economy be developed further?

_____

_____

_____

Name _____ Class _____ Date _____

Word Wise

Word Bank Choose one word from the word bank to fill in each blank. When you have finished, you will have a short summary of important ideas from the section.

Word Bank

isthmus   biodiversity
tourism   deforestation
hurricanes

Central America is located on a(n) _____ that is rich in

_____. However, _____ has seriously

reduced the number of native plants and animals in the region.

Although Central America has its share of natural disasters such as

_____, many people vacation in Central American countries.

As a result, _____ contributes to the economies of these

nations. Plantations, or large commercial farms, are another important part

of the region's economy.

Name _____ Class _____ Date _____

Take Notes

Map Skills Use the maps in your book to make a key and to label the Places to Know on the outline map below.

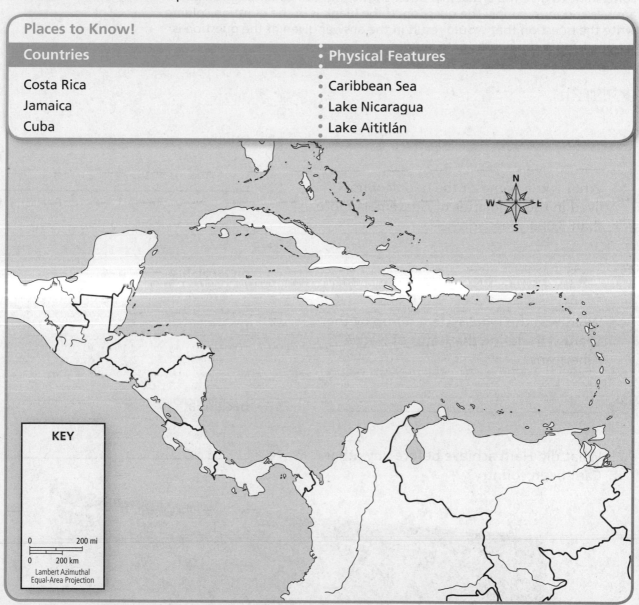

Places to Know!

Countries	Physical Features
Costa Rica	Caribbean Sea
Jamaica	Lake Nicaragua
Cuba	Lake Aititlán

KEY

```
0          200 mi
0          200 km
Lambert Azimuthal
Equal-Area Projection
```

Essential Question

How might the frequency of natural disasters affect a country's ability to be independent?

_____

_____

_____

Word Wise

Vocabulary Quiz Show Some quiz shows ask a question and expect the contestant to give the answer. In other shows, the contestant is given an answer and must supply the question. If the blank is in the question column, write the question that would result in the answer given. If the question is supplied, write the appropriate answer.

QUESTION

① _____

② What is the name of the people who lived in the highlands of Guatemala more than 3,000 years ago?

③ _____

④ What was the legal system set up by the Spanish to define the status of Native Americans?

⑤ _____

⑥ What did Haiti achieve before any other Caribbean country?

ANSWER

① colony

② _____

③ dictatorship

④ _____

⑤ hacienda

⑥ _____

Name _____ Class _____ Date _____

Take Notes

Cause and Effect In this section you read how Spanish colonists established the encomienda system. Use the graphic organizer below to show the effects of this system on the region's Native Americans, Africans, and Spaniards.

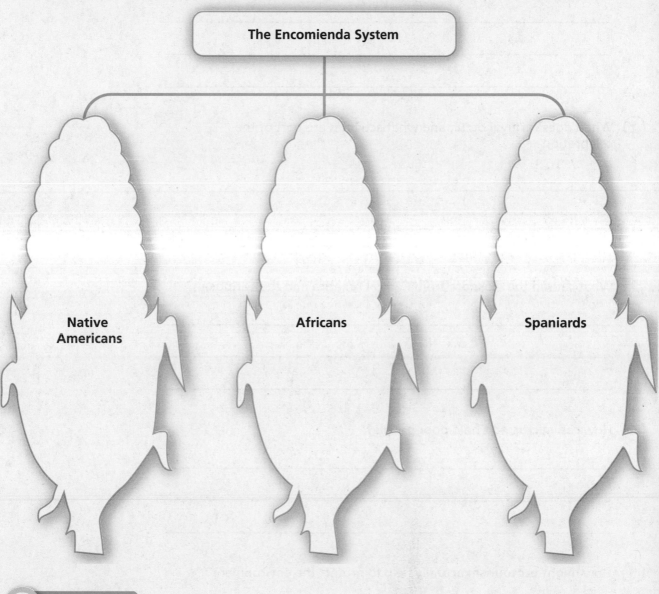

The Encomienda System

Native Americans

Africans

Spaniards

Essential Question

Were the Spanish colonists independent or interdependent?

_____

_____

_____

Word Wise

Words In Context For each question below, write an answer that shows your understanding of the boldfaced key term.

1 What beliefs does **Santeria** combine?

_____

_____

_____

2 When does **carnival** occur, and what activities are part of the celebration?

_____

_____

_____

3 What caused the **diaspora** from Central America and the Caribbean?

_____

_____

_____

4 How can **microcredit** help poor people?

_____

_____

_____

5 How might **ecotourism** actually help to protect the environment?

_____

_____

_____

Name _____   Class _____   Date _____

Take Notes

Summarize Use the web below to summarize what you have learned about the governments and economies of present-day Central America and the Caribbean. For the top section, fill in information about the different governments in the area. For the bottom section, fill in information about the different economies in the region.

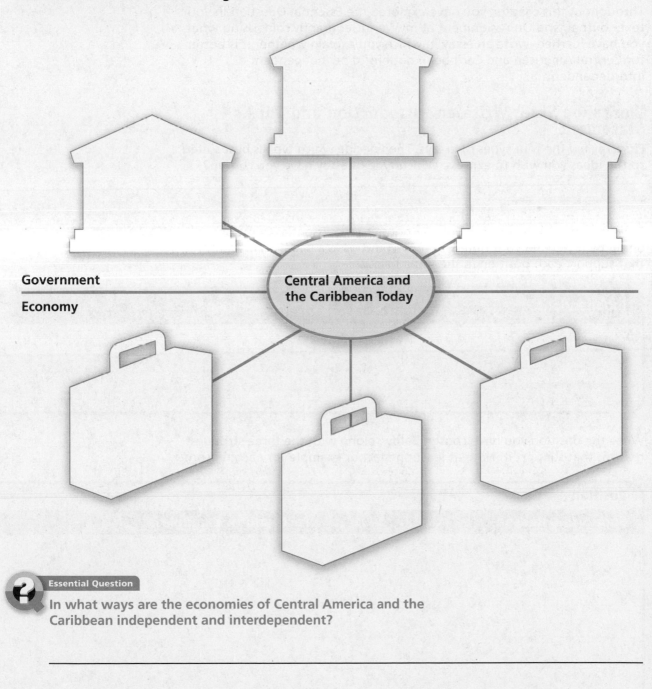

Government

Economy

Central America and the Caribbean Today

Essential Question

In what ways are the economies of Central America and the Caribbean independent and interdependent?

_____

_____

_____

Essential Question   Writer's Workshop

Is it better to be independent or interdependent?

Prepare to Write

Throughout this chapter, you have explored the Essential Question in your text, journal, and On Assignment at myWorldGeography.com. Using what you have learned, write an essay in which you explain whether it is better for Central American and Caribbean nations to be independent or interdependent.

Workshop Skill: Write an Introduction and Thesis Statement

First, review the four types of essays. Then decide which type is best suited to the ideas you wish to express. Which type of essay have you chosen?

_____

Develop your thesis, which is your response to the Essential Question. Begin by reviewing your notes. To help you choose a position, list reasons that support each position in the table below.

Independent	Interdependent

Write the position you have chosen below, along with the three strongest reasons that support it. Note at least one fact or example for each reason.

Position	
Supporting Reasons	**Facts and/or Examples**

Write Your Thesis Statement

Your thesis statement states your position and three reasons that support it. The thesis statement will be the last sentence(s) in your introductory paragraph. For example: *Independence is essential for Central American and Caribbean nations because*

_____, _____, and _____.

If your sentence is too long, place your reasons in a second sentence. For example: *Independence is essential for Central American and Caribbean countries. This is true because*

_____, _____, and _____.

Now write your thesis statement:

_____

Write Your Introduction

The first paragraph of an essay introduces the topic to the reader. An introduction has three parts:

1. A statement indicating what the essay is about.

Example *Independence and interdependence are characteristics that*

_____.

2. An indication of why the subject or issue is important.

Example *Understanding a particular nation's independence or*

interdependence is essential to understanding _____.

3. A thesis statement.

Write your introductory sentence: _____.

State the issue's importance: _____.

Write your thesis statement, including three supporting arguments:

_____

Draft Your Essay

Introduction: Rewrite your introductory paragraph on your own paper.
Body Paragraphs: Develop each argument to support your position in a separate paragraph. Include details and examples.
Conclusion: Summarize your arguments. When you have finished, proofread your essay.

Name _____ Class _____ Date _____

Is conflict unavoidable?

Preview Before you begin this chapter, think about the Essential Question. Understanding how the Essential Question connects to your life will help you understand the chapter you are about to read.

Connect to Your Life

1 What has caused conflicts in your family, school, community, or state? Name two recent conflicts.

_____

_____

2 Listed in the table below are three reasons for conflicts. Rate how apt each one is to cause conflict, with 1 being likely and 5 being unlikely. To help decide, you may want to consider the conflicts you named.

Reason for Conflict	How likely is it to cause conflict?				
Misunderstandings	1	2	3	4	5
Power struggles	1	2	3	4	5
Differences	1	2	3	4	5
Other: _____	1	2	3	4	5

Connect to the Chapter

3 Now think about sources of conflict in a country or region that can lead to tension (such as differences in economic opportunity). Preview the chapter by skimming the its headings, photographs, and graphics. In the web below, predict sources of conflict.

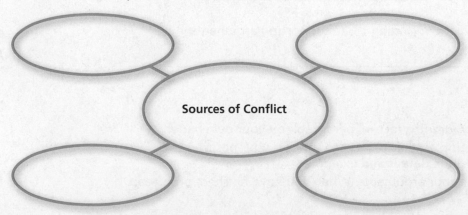

Sources of Conflict

4 After you read the chapter, return to this page. Use a highlighter to mark your accurate predictions.

Name _____ Class _____ Date _____

Connect to myStory: Daniella's Coffee Run

(1) Describe at least two things that you can do to get along with other students.

_____

_____

_____

(2) Think of the things that Daniella does to get along with different people that she meets during her workday. Write your ideas in the appropriate row below.

People Daniella Meets	Things She Does to Get Along
Tourists	
Merchants	

(3) Do you think that Daniella's efforts to get along are helpful to her and to other people? Explain.

_____

_____

_____

_____

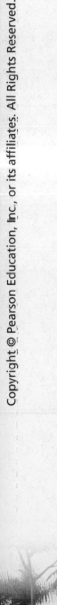

97

Word Wise

Word Map Follow the model below to make a word map. The key term *ecosystem* is in the center oval. Write the definition in your own words at the upper left. In the upper right, list Characteristics, which means words or phrases that relate to the term. At the lower left list Noncharacteristics, which means words and phrases that would not be associated with it. In the lower right, draw a picture of the key term or use it in a sentence.

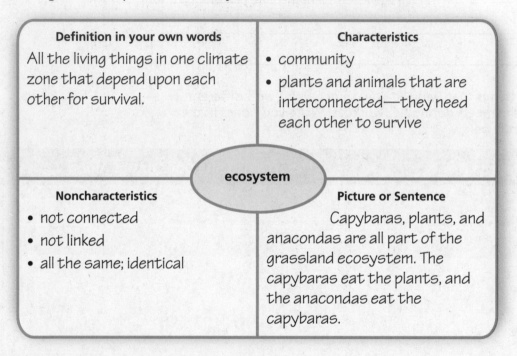

Definition in your own words
All the living things in one climate zone that depend upon each other for survival.

Characteristics
- community
- plants and animals that are interconnected—they need each other to survive

ecosystem

Noncharacteristics
- not connected
- not linked
- all the same; identical

Picture or Sentence
Capybaras, plants, and anacondas are all part of the grassland ecosystem. The capybaras eat the plants, and the anacondas eat the capybaras.

Now use the word map below to explore the meaning of the word *cordillera*. You may use your student text, a dictionary, and/or a thesaurus to complete each of the four sections.

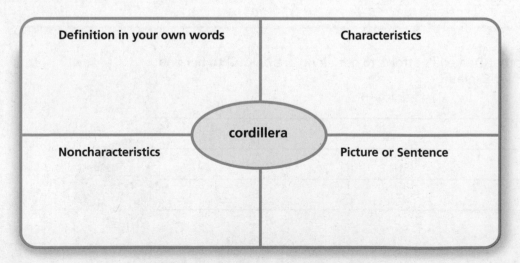

Definition in your own words

Characteristics

cordillera

Noncharacteristics

Picture or Sentence

Make word maps of your own on a separate piece of paper for these words: *Llanos* and *terraced farming*.

98

Name _____   Class _____   Date _____

Take Notes

Map Skills Use the maps in your book to make a key and to label the Places to Know on the outline map below.

Places to Know!

Physical Features	Cities
Cordillera Occidental	Bogotá
Guiana Highlands	Caracas
Orinoco River	Georgetown
Llanos	Cayenne

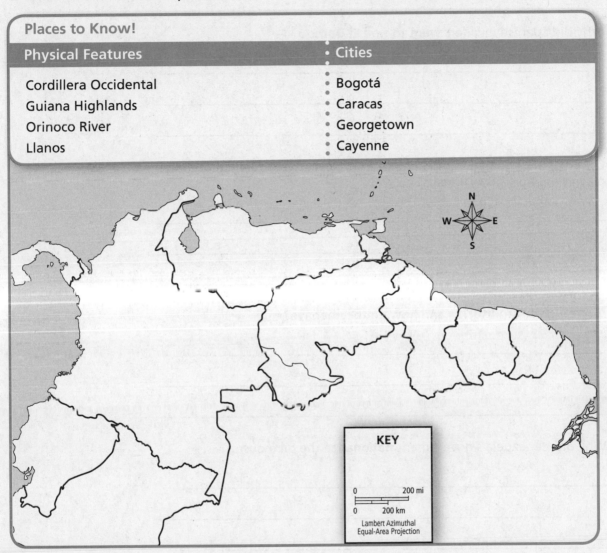

KEY

0 _____ 200 mi

0 _____ 200 km

Lambert Azimuthal
Equal-Area Projection

Essential Question

How might geography be a divisive force in the region?

_____

_____

_____

Word Wise

Words In Context For each question below, write an answer that shows your understanding of the boldfaced key term.

(1) Why did Spanish invaders want to find **El Dorado**?

_____

_____

_____

(2) Once the area gained independence from Spain, what role did **caudillos** play in the new governments?

_____

_____

_____

(3) What are **paramilitaries** and how do they behave?

_____

_____

_____

(4) Why did Venezuela's government **nationalize** the oil industry?

_____

_____

_____

(5) What was the purpose of Pérez's **austerity measures** in Venezuela?

_____

_____

_____

Name _____ Class _____ Date _____

Take Notes

Main Ideas and Details Use what you have read about the history of
Caribbean South America to complete the graphic organizer below. Find
the topic heading in the chapter. Write its main idea in your own words.
Then give two details that support it.

Topic: Cultures Collide

Main Idea:

Details:

1.

2.

Topic: The Fight for Independence

Main Idea:

Details:

1.

2.

Topic: After Independence

Main Idea:

Details:

1.

2.

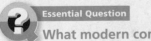 **Essential Question**

What modern conflicts in Caribbean South America have their
roots in colonial history?

_____

_____

_____

Word Wise

Vocabulary Quiz Show Some quiz shows ask a question and expect the contestant to give the answer. In other shows, the contestant is given an answer and must supply the question. If the blank is in the question column, write the question that would result in the answer given. If the question is supplied, write the appropriate answer.

QUESTION

(1) What do you call it when land sinks?

(2) _____

(3) What word describes a person who rebels against the government?

(4) _____

ANSWER

(1) _____

(2) representative democracy

(3) _____

(4) Latin America

Name _____ Class _____ Date _____

Take Notes

Compare and Contrast Caribbean South America has great diversity. At the same time, the nations of the region have much in common. Fill in the table below to describe how parts of the region are alike and different.

	Similarities	Differences
Cultures		
Environmental issues		
Governments		

Essential Question

What issues fuel conflicts in Caribbean South America?

_____

_____

_____

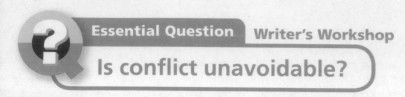

Essential Question **Writer's Workshop**

Is conflict unavoidable?

Prepare to Write

Throughout this chapter, you have explored the Essential Question in your text, journal, and On Assignment at myWorldGeography.com. Use what you've learned to write an essay on whether or not conflict is avoidable in Caribbean South America. Include information about tensions from racial and ethnic differences, the various governments, and religious and linguistic diversity. Also keep in mind how the region's history led to another source of conflict: differences in economic and social opportunity.

Workshop Skill: Write Body Paragraphs

Review the first steps of drafting an essay: writing a thesis statement and an introduction. Remember that your thesis statement presents the main point of your essay. Here's an example thesis statement: *Conflict in Caribbean South America may be avoidable due to efforts to reduce the causes of tension.*

Three body paragraphs should come between the introduction and conclusion in a five-paragraph essay. Each paragraph should develop one of the three ideas from your introduction. Each of the three paragraphs should contain: (1) a topic sentence; (2) details and evidence to help you make your point; and (3) a concluding sentence.

Write Your Topic Sentence Each body paragraph should begin with a topic sentence. A topic sentence serves two purposes: to state the main idea of the paragraph and to act as a transition from the paragraph before.

Sample Topic Sentence *Colonial oppression of Native Americans and slaves led to inequalities that still persist today.*

Support Your Topic Sentence Use details and explanations to support your topic sentence. Supporting details may include facts, quotations, examples, and other evidence. These supporting details help to prove that your ideas are correct. After each supporting detail, you may want to add a second sentence that discusses the idea.

Supporting Detail *There is a huge gap between rich and poor throughout the region.*

Supporting Discussion *A small minority has owned most of the land and wealth, which has led to civil conflict.*

Supporting Detail *In Columbia, paramilitary groups have fought to maintain privileges and power for the few, while rebel groups have fought for change for the many.*

Additional Supporting Detail *In Venezuela, the government has tried to close the gap by nationalizing the oil industry.*

End With a Concluding Sentence Wrap up each paragraph with a concluding sentence that ties together your supporting details.

Concluding Sentence *Efforts to correct imbalances have lead to gradual improvements, along with increased communication between opposing groups.*

Write a Body Paragraph Now write your own body paragraph for your essay. You may want to completely fill in the outline given below, or you may have a shorter paragraph.

Topic Sentence _____

_____

Supporting Detail _____

_____

Supporting Discussion _____

_____

Supporting Detail _____

_____

Supporting Discussion _____

_____

Supporting Detail _____

_____

Supporting Discussion _____

_____

Concluding Sentence _____

_____

Draft Your Essay

Use the body paragraph above in your complete essay. Write it on your own paper. Be sure that each of your body paragraphs has a topic sentence, supporting details, and a concluding sentence.

Name _____ Class _____ Date _____

What are the challenges of diversity?

Preview Before you begin this chapter, think about the Essential Question. Understanding how the Essential Question connects to your life will help you understand the chapter you are about to read.

Connect to Your Life

(1) Think about the wide range of differences in the likes and dislikes of a group of people. For example, you may like pizza prepared one way and a friend may like it with different toppings. Think about some general ways that in which people express their differences in taste. Fill in the table below with your ideas.

Categories	Clothing	Food	Music	Interests
Expressions of Different Taste				

(2) Do some differences in taste encourage or discourage interaction with other groups? Explain.

_____

_____

Connect to the Chapter

(3) Preview the chapter by skimming the chapter's headings, photographs, and graphics. In the table below, predict the kind of challenges that diversity might present to the people of the Andes and the Pampas. An example is given in the linguistic category. Fill in a prediction of your own in each of the other columns.

Types of Diversity	Ethnic	Religious	Political	Linguistic
Challenges				When people do not share a language, they may have trouble communicating.

(4) After you read the chapter, return to your predictions above. Did anything you learned about diversity in the Andes and Pampas surprise you? Explain.

_____

_____

Name _____ Class _____ Date _____

Connect to myStory: Under the Rich Mountain

(**1**) Think of high school students you know who have part-time jobs. How do their jobs differ from Omar's job?

_____

_____

(**2**) In the diagram below, list details from Omar's story about the effects of Cerro Mountain on life in Bolivia.

(**3**) Think about Omar's story. What kinds of resources are mentioned? Write your predictions of how mining has affected this area.

_____

_____

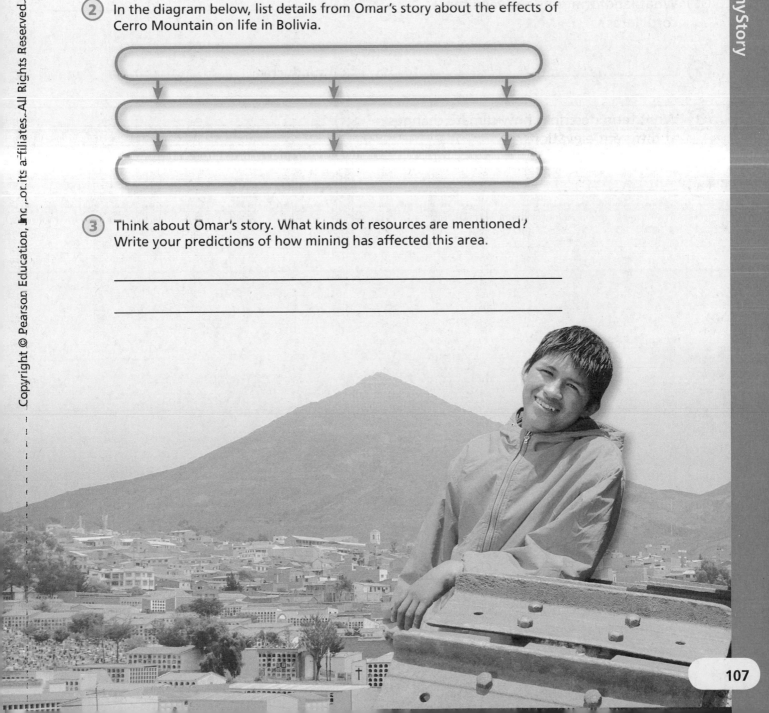

Name _____ Class _____ Date _____

Word Wise

Vocabulary Quiz Show Some quiz shows ask a question and expect the contestant to give the answer. In other shows, the contestant is given an answer and must supply the question. If the blank is in the question column, write the question that would result in the answer given. If the question is supplied, write the appropriate answer.

QUESTION	ANSWER
(1) What landform runs between the cordilleras?	(1) _____
(2) _____	(2) subducted
(3) What term describes how climate changes at different elevations?	(3) _____
(4) _____	(4) El Niño

Name _____ Class _____ Date _____

Take Notes

Map Skills Use the maps in your book to make a key and to label the Places to Know on the outline map below.

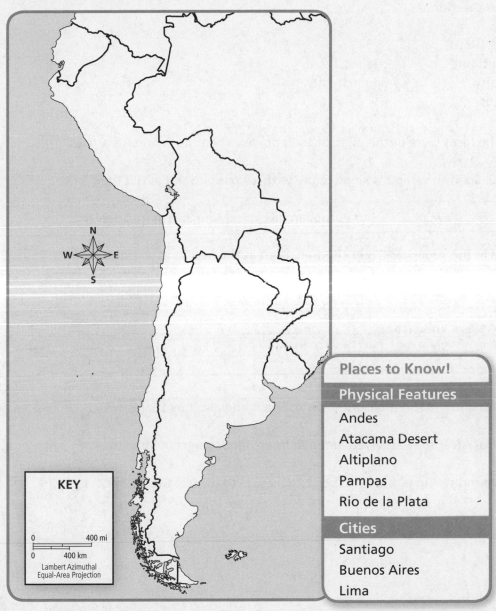

KEY

0   400 mi

0   400 km

Lambert Azimuthal
Equal-Area Projection

Places to Know!

Physical Features

Andes

Atacama Desert

Altiplano

Pampas

Rio de la Plata

Cities

Santiago

Buenos Aires

Lima

Essential Question

How does the geographic diversity of the region determine where people live?

_____

_____

_____

Name _____ Class _____ Date _____

Word Wise

Word Bank Choose one word from the word bank to fill in each blank. When you have finished, you will have a short summary of important ideas from the section.

Word Bank

mercantilism   criollos
immunity   oligarchy
mestizos

The Incas were at the peak of their power when the Spaniards arrived

in 1532. Spanish weapons killed many of these people, and so did their lack

of _____ to European diseases. More and more Spaniards

settled in the Americas. Their children, born in the new land, were called

_____. The offspring of Spanish men and indigenous

women were known as _____.

Under the economic system of _____, the

colonists had to send their resources to Spain and also buy Spanish

products. After they achieved independence, landowners of Spanish

background set up a(n) _____ to control the nation.

Name _____ Class _____ Date _____

Take Notes

Cause and Effect Use what you have read about the history of the Andes and the Pampas to state what caused new people to come to the region and what effect they had on the region.

	Spanish Conquistadors	Immigrants in 1800s
Why did they come?		
What happened after they arrived?		

Essential Question

How has the history of the region contributed to its ethnic diversity?

_____

_____

_____

Word Wise

Words In Context For each question below, write an answer that shows your understanding of the boldfaced key term.

1. Why is a **diversified economy** beneficial for the nations of the Andes and Pampas?

   _____

   _____

   _____

2. What is the purpose of the **MERCOSUR** trading bloc?

   _____

   _____

   _____

3. Why might the government of Bolivia want to improve its citizens' **literacy**?

   _____

   _____

   _____

4. When would a **referendum** be used in a democracy?

   _____

   _____

   _____

5. Why did the people of Chile vote to **amend** their constitution?

   _____

   _____

   _____

Name _____ Class _____ Date _____

Take Notes

Summarize Use what you have read about the Andes and the Pampas today
to fill in the key ideas from this section of the chapter in the table below.

	Key Ideas
Cultures	
Environmental Problems	
Economies	
Governments	

Essential Question

**In what ways have nations in the region tried
to diversify their economies?**

_____

_____

_____

Name _____ Class _____ Date _____

What are the challenges of diversity?

Prepare to Write

Throughout this chapter, you have explored the Essential Question in your text, journal, and On Assignment at myWorldGeography.com. Use what you've learned to write an essay describing the challenges that diversity has caused in the Andes and the Pampas.

Workshop Skill: Write a Conclusion

Review how to draft an essay. Drafting requires writing a thesis statement, an introduction, three body paragraphs, and a conclusion. The conclusion wraps up your essay and brings everything together.

Writing a strong conclusion requires thought and effort. Remember, it is the last impression that your essay makes on your readers.

Preparing to Write Your Conclusion   Before you write your conclusion, reread your essay. Think about your thesis, including the main ideas and details that support it. What new questions spring to mind? What related topic might you want to investigate at another time? Does the topic of diversity affect you personally? After you reread, brainstorm some responses to your new questions.

Use a Checklist   When you're ready to write your conclusion, do so in an organized way. Follow a checklist like the one below. As you complete each task, check it off your list.

_____ Restate your thesis to remind the reader of the whole point of your essay.

_____ Summarize the most important ideas that support your thesis.

_____ Include a few sentences that add something new to your topic.

_____ Explain the importance of your topic and suggest its deeper meaning.

What Makes a Strong Conclusion?   A strong conclusion should tie together the different strands of your essay. It should give your reader the feeling that everything adds up and makes sense. At the same time, your conclusion should be interesting, thought-provoking, and unique.

Sample Conclusion Here are some sample sentences that could be used to form a cohesive conclusion:

- Restatement of the Thesis *The region's mountains and grasslands shaped its history and led to great diversity.*

- Summary of an Important Idea *The gold and silver of the highlands attracted the conquistadors, who were followed by colonists and other immigrants.*

- A New Idea *If the region had not been so rich in silver and gold, its history might have been very different.*

- Why This Topic Is Important *Learning about the diversity of the region helps us to understand the problems the people in this region face today.*

Write Your Conclusion

Now write your own concluding paragraph for your essay.

Restatement of the Thesis _____

_____

_____

Summary of One Important Idea _____

_____

Summary of Another Important Idea _____

_____

Summary of One Important Idea _____

_____

A New Idea _____

_____

Why This Topic Is Important _____

_____

_____

Draft Your Essay

Use the concluding paragraph above in your completed essay. Write your essay on another sheet of paper.

Name _____ Class _____ Date _____

Who should benefit from a country's resources?

Preview Before you begin this chapter, think about the Essential Question. Understanding how the Essential Question connects to your life will help you understand the chapter you are about to read.

Connect to Your Life

(1) How do you and your friends share? Think about sharing a bag of hard candies. What are the positives and negatives of different ways of sharing? List your ideas in the table below.

Different Ways to Share			
Sharing/ Strategy	Equal portion for all	Biggest appetite gets more	More for those who pay more	Other
Pros			
Cons			

(2) Why do people disagree about which sharing method is the best?

_____

_____

Connect to the Chapter

(3) Now think about different ways that a country's resources might be distributed among citizens. For example, poor citizens might not benefit from a country's oil reserves. Preview the chapter by skimming the headings, photographs and illustrations.

(4) Read the chapter. Think of how groups in Brazil have shared resources during its history in the ways shown in the table below. Write yes or no in the first row. For those columns in which the answer is yes, write the name of the group that used it in the second row.

Ways to Divide Resources in the Real World		
Sharing/ Strategy	Shares are based on need.	Rich/powerful people take more than others.	Everybody fights.
Ever used in Brazil?		
Name (if yes)		

Name _____ Class _____ Date _____

Connect to myStory: Vinicius's Game Plan

(1) Do you think that teenagers should set goals for the future? Why or why not?

_____

_____

_____

(2) What is Vinicius doing to reach his goals? What obstacles, or problems, does he face?

Goal 1: Become a professional soccer player (Plan A)
Things he is doing
Obstacles

Goal 2: Go to the university (Plan B)
Things he is doing
Obstacles

(3) Do you think that Vinicius's goals will help him have a better future in Brazil? Why or why not?

_____

_____

_____

_____

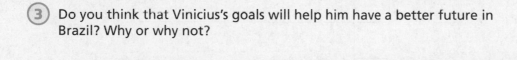

Word Wise

Crossword Puzzle The clues describe key terms from this section. Fill in the numbered *Across* boxes with the correct key terms. Then, do the same with the *Down* clues.

Across	Down
1. the topmost level of a rain forest	3. the land area that drains into the Amazon River
2. The Cerrado in the Brazilian Highlands is a vast _____.	4. a Brazilian slum

Name _____ Class _____ Date _____

Take Notes

Map Skills Use the maps in your book to make a key and to label the Places
to Know on the outline map below.

Places to Know!

Physical Features	· Cities
Amazon River	· São Paulo
Pantanal	· Rio de Janeiro
Cerrado	
Guiana Highlands	

KEY

0   400 mi

0   400 km

Lambert Azimuthal
Equal-Area Projection

Essential Question

Where are some of Brazil's resources located? Explain.

_____

_____

_____

Word Wise

Sentence Builder Complete the sentences using the information you learned in this section. Include terminal punctuation.

(1) **Brazilwood** is different from other kinds of wood because _____

_____

(2) The main feature of an **export economy** is _____

_____

(3) **"Boom and bust" cycles** in an economy are the opposite of "steady and even" cycles because _____

_____

(4) An **abolitionist** is interested in _____

_____

(5) When leaders worry about a **coup**, they fear _____

_____

Name _____ Class _____ Date _____

Take Notes

Sequence Use what you have read about the history of Brazil to complete the table below by filling in the missing date or event in each row.

Date	Important Events in Brazilian History
1494	The Treaty of Tordesillas gives Portugal colonization rights to Brazil.
1500	
	Portugal's royal family flees to Brazil.
1822	Brazil becomes an empire under Pedro I.
1888	
	Brazil becomes an independent republic.
	Dictator Getúlio Vargas overthrows the government.

Essential Question

Did the export of sugar and other valuable resources from Brazil benefit all the people in the colony? Explain.

_____

_____

_____

Name _____ Class _____ Date _____

Word Wise

Vocabulary Quiz Show Some quiz shows ask a question and expect the contestant to give the answer. In other shows, the contestant is given an answer and must supply the question. If the blank is in the question column, write the question that would result in the answer given. If the question is supplied, write the appropriate answer.

QUESTION

ANSWER

① What do you call the deliberate designing of a city?

① _____

② _____

② ethanol

③ What is the financial system in which the government does *not* set prices?

③ _____

④ _____

④ social services

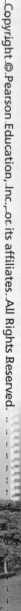

Name _____ Class _____ Date _____

Take Notes

Summarize Use what you have read about Brazil today to complete the
table below. Under each heading, write at least two important ideas or
details that sum up what that subsection is about.

A Rich Culture
1.
2.

Environmental Issues
1.
2.

A Growing Economy
1.
2.

Government for the People
1.
2.

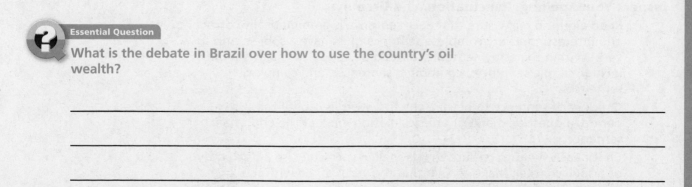

Essential Question

**What is the debate in Brazil over how to use the country's oil
wealth?**

_____

_____

_____

Essential Question Writer's Workshop

Who should benefit from a country's resources?

Prepare to Write

Throughout this chapter, you have explored the Essential Question in your text, journal, and On Assignment at myWorldGeography.com. Use what you've learned to write an essay about who has benefited from Brazil's resources—and whether the division of resources is fair. Include information about the resources of the Amazon basin, the country's minerals, Brazil's boom and bust cycles, and the country's early economies based on sugar and coffee. You may want to add how the Portuguese legacy has affected the division of resources.

Workshop Skill: Revise Your Essay

Revising involves carefully reading over a draft of your essay to make it better. Revising comes *after* the first two steps of the writing process: (1) prewriting, and (2) drafting, when you develop and write your thesis statement, an introduction, at least three body paragraphs, and a conclusion.

In this lesson, you will learn more about revising. During this step, you will look closely at each part of your essay and at the paragraphs that make up each part. You will also focus on the individual sentences and words.

Improve Each Part of Your Essay

Use this checklist to revise your essay. As you complete each task, check it off.

_____ **The introduction** is the first impression you make on your readers. It should be clear and interesting. Your thesis statement should not be too general or too specific.

_____ **Each paragraph in the body** of your essay should have a main idea and several supporting details. Each paragraph should be logical and easy to follow.

_____ **The transitions** from one paragraph to the next should make sense.

_____ **The conclusion** is the final impression you make on your readers. It should be clear and interesting. It should be based on information from your essay.

Inspect Your Spelling, Punctuation, and Grammar

_____ **Read aloud** to make sure that each sentence is grammatically correct and interesting. Every complete sentence must have a subject and a verb. Within the essay, sentences should be varied. An essay should include simple sentences, compound sentences, and complex sentences.

_____ **Check each sentence** to be sure the first word is capitalized. Use a period, a question mark, or an exclamation mark at the end of each sentence.

_____ **Check each word** to be sure that is spelled correctly. Use a dictionary or a spell checker. Make certain that the verbs agree with the subjects. Capitalize the names of people and places.

Use Proofreading Marks

Proofreading Marks

⟂ capitalize	⊙ period
¶ start new paragraph	⟩ insert a comma
roͨk insert	ℓ delete

Here is a sample of a short paragraph that has been proofread. Changes have also been made to increase sentence variety.

¶ The mountins and forests of brazil hold amazing resources. The forests produce fruits, nuts, rubber, pam oil an timber. In the highlands, brazil has great minral wealth. There is iron or, bauxite, and gold. During the 1500s, Portuguese traders set up an expart economy to profit from these resources.

Practice Revision

Revise the following paragraph. Use proofreading marks to show errors in capitalization, spelling, and end punctuation. Then, on the lines below, combine the two underlined sentences to improve sentence length and variety.

Portugal profited grately from the resources of brazil. First, they set up

trading posts They began exporting brazilwood. It was used for dye. They

added sugar, coffe, gold, and diamonds to their exports the native peoples

and the African slaves suffered under this unair system.

_____

_____

Revise Your Essay

Use the checklists given in this workshop and proofreading marks to revise your own essay. Then, rewrite your final draft on a new piece of paper.

Name _____ Class _____ Date _____

Essential Question

What are the challenges of diversity?

Preview Before you begin this chapter, think about the Essential Question. Understanding how the Essential Question connects to your life will help you understand the chapter you are about to read.

Connect to Your Life

1. Think of a time when you learned about another culture. Name the other culture and tell at least one way in which it differed from yours.

   _____

   _____

2. Think about some general ways that in which people express their differences in taste. Fill in the table below with your ideas.

Categories	Clothing	Food	Music	Interests
Expressions of Different Taste				

Connect to the Chapter

3. Preview the chapter. Skim the headings, photos, and graphics. In the table below, predict the challenges that diversity presented to the people living in ancient and medieval Europe. One example is given in the table.

Type of Diversity	Ethnic	Religious	Political	Linguistic
Challenges			People with different values have different political viewpoints. The values and political ideas may actually be exact opposites.	

4. After reading the chapter, put a check mark next to your ideas that turned out to be correct.

Name _____   Class _____   Date _____

Connect to myStory: Alexander the Great: A Prophecy Fulfilled

(1) List the major events in your life up to now. You should write at least three.

_____

_____

_____

(2) List the major events of Alexander's life in the boxes of the chart.

The Life of Alexander the Great

Growing Up   **Fighting Persia**   **Building an Empire**

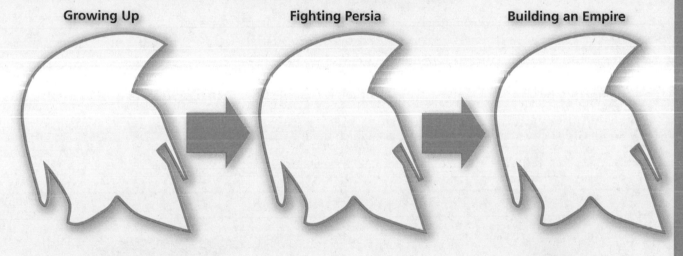

(3) Look at the Growing Up box above. How do your life events differ from Alexander's early life events?

_____

_____

_____

(4) What might be the challenges of ruling an empire as big and diverse as the one Alexander the Great conquered?

_____

_____

_____

_____

Word Wise

Sentence Builder Complete the sentences using the information you learned in this section. Include terminal punctuation.

1. Greece is considered a **cultural hearth** because _____

   _____

2. Greek scholars started a branch of study called **philosophy** which

   _____

3. Two of the most famous Greek **city-states** were _____

   _____

4. In Athens, the male citizens took part in the world's first **direct**

   democracy by _____

5. Some Greek city-states were **oligarchies**, which means _____

   _____

Name _____ Class _____ Date _____

Take Notes

Map Skills Use the maps in *all* sections of this chapter to make a key and to label the Places to Know on the outline map below. Remember, in addition to this section, you will need to refer to Sections 2 through 4.

Places to Know!

Physical Features	Countries/Empires	City-States and Cities
Aegean Sea	Spain	Athens
Crete	Italy	Sparta
Peloponnesian Peninsula	Holy Roman Empire	Constantinople
Mediterranean Sea	France	Rome
Balkan Peninsula		Venice
Black Sea		

KEY

0 _____ 400 mi

0 _____ 400 km

Lambert Conformal Conic Projection

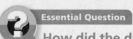

Essential Question

How did the diversity of Alexander the Great's Empire affect Greek culture?

_____

_____

_____

Word Wise

Word Map Follow the model below to make a word map. The key term *patrician* is in the center oval. Write the definition in your own words at the upper left. In the upper right, list Characteristics, which means words or phrases that relate to the term. At the lower left list Noncharacteristics, which means words and phrases that would not be associated with it. In the lower right, draw a picture of the key term or use it in a sentence.

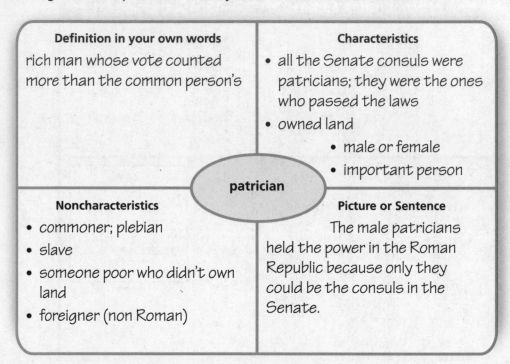

Definition in your own words
rich man whose vote counted more than the common person's

Characteristics
- all the Senate consuls were patricians; they were the ones who passed the laws
- owned land
    - male or female
    - important person

patrician

Noncharacteristics
- commoner; plebian
- slave
- someone poor who didn't own land
- foreigner (non Roman)

Picture or Sentence
The male patricians held the power in the Roman Republic because only they could be the consuls in the Senate.

Now use the word map below to explore the meaning of the key term *representative democracy.* You may use your student text, a dictionary, and/or a thesaurus to complete each of the four sections.

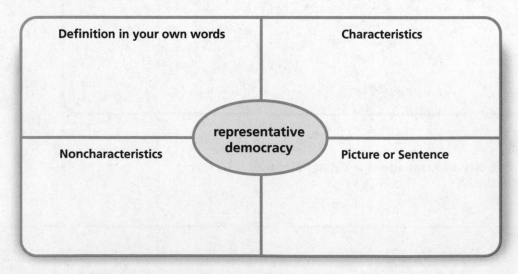

Definition in your own words

Characteristics

representative democracy

Noncharacteristics

Picture or Sentence

Make word maps of your own on a separate piece of paper for these key terms: *Pax Romana* and *aqueduct.*

Name _____ Class _____ Date _____

Take Notes

Sequence Record major events from the history of Ancient Rome on the timeline below. Check the section to be sure you are putting the events in chronological order.

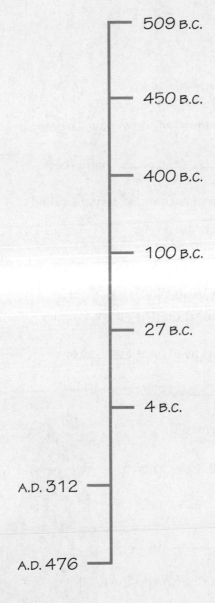

509 B.C.

450 B.C.

400 B.C.

100 B.C.

27 B.C.

4 B.C.

A.D. 312

A.D. 476

Essential Question

How did the Romans use citizenship to unify a diverse empire?

_____

_____

_____

Word Wise

Word Bank Choose one word from the word bank to fill in each blank. When you have finished, you will have a short summary of important ideas from the section.

Word Bank

Schism	lords
vassals	feudalism
manorialism	

In Western Europe, a ruler named Charlemagne (742–814) gave large

pieces of land as estates to nobles called _____, who then

owed him services. This was the start of a system of exchanged services called

_____.

The nobles who received estates then gave part of their land to

_____ in exchange for their protection. They were knights

that gave military support to the nobles. Peasants lived on these estates

under the economic system called _____. In this system,

peasants worked the land for the nobles who owned it.

Meanwhile, in the Byzantine empire, the Christian church

developed differently from the Church in Rome. The two

churches split apart in the Great _____ of 1054.

After the division, there was the Roman Catholic Church and the

Greek Orthodox Church.

Name _____ Class _____ Date _____

Take Notes

Summarize Use the information in your textbook to complete this graphic organizer. In the top three boxes, record details about the roles that the king, the lords, and the vassals played in feudalism. Then in the bottom box, write a few sentences summarizing how the system of feudalism worked.

King

_____

_____

_____

Lords

_____

_____

_____

Vassals

_____

_____

_____

How Feudalism Worked

_____

_____

_____

Essential Question

How did cultural differences between the East and the West affect the Christian church?

_____

_____

_____

Name _____ Class _____ Date _____

Word Wise

Words In Context For each question below, write an answer that shows your understanding of the boldfaced key term.

(1) Why did the craftspeople form **guilds**?

_____

_____

_____

(2) What did the Catholic Church hope that the **Crusades** would accomplish?

_____

_____

_____

(3) Who started the **Reconquista**, and what was its purpose?

_____

_____

_____

(4) How did the **Magna Carta** affect English government?

_____

_____

_____

Name _____ Class _____ Date _____

Take Notes

Cause and Effect Use this cause-and-effect graphic organizer to record information about the Crusades and the decline of feudalism.

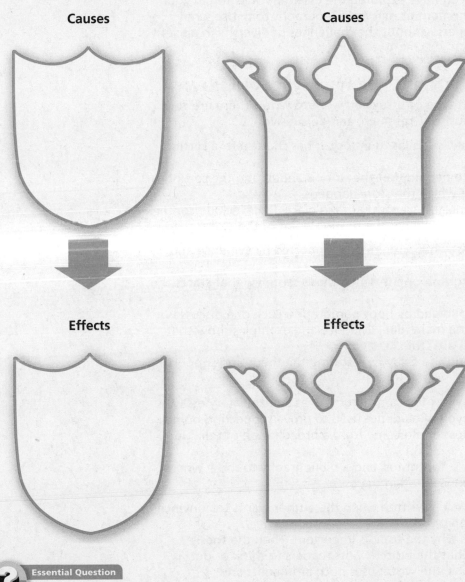

The Crusades

Causes

Decline of Feudalism

Causes

Effects

Effects

Essential Question

How did diversity have both positive and negative effects on Spain?

_____

_____

_____

? Essential Question   Writer's Workshop

What are the challenges of diversity?

Prepare to Write

Throughout this chapter, you have explored the Essential Question in your text, journal, and On Assignment at myWorldGeography.com. Use what you've learned to write an essay about the challenges of diversity in ancient or medieval Europe.

Workshop Skill: Understand the Four Types of Essays

First you must decide what type of essay you want to write. There are four essay types: narrative, expository, research, and persuasive.

Narrative Essay This essay is similar to a story. It has characters, a setting, and a plot.
- The characters are the people that the story is about, and the setting is the time and place in which the story happens.
- The plot is the sequence of events that take place. Plots include conflict and lead up to a climax, which is the turning point of the story.

Expository Essay This essay has a main idea supported by evidence and examples.
- An introductory paragraph opens with a thesis sentence that states the main idea.
- The introduction is followed by body paragraphs. Each one discusses a point that supports the main idea. Evidence and examples show that the supporting points are true.
- The conclusion sums up the essay by restating the thesis and supporting points.

Research Essay This essay has the same structure as an expository essay. The difference lies in the type of evidence used to prove supporting points.
- Evidence and examples should come from a broad range of reliable sources.
- Writers use quotations, footnotes, and a bibliography to show where they located the evidence used in the essay.

Persuasive Essay This essay is written when the author wants to convince readers to adopt an opinion or take action.
- The introduction tells why the topic is important. Then the thesis statement explains what the writer wants readers to think or do.
- In the body paragraphs, the writer uses both arguments and evidence to prove the supporting points.
- The conclusion reviews the main points and urges the reader to adopt the opinion or take the action mentioned.

Identify Essay Types Use what you have learned to identify the different essay types. Read the four descriptions in the table on the next page. In the column on the right, write if the essay described is a narrative, expository, research, or persuasive one.

136

Essay Description	Type
1. The essay urges people of different cultures to stop fighting and learn from each other. It offers examples of people who have gained new insights from other cultures.	_____
2. The essay examines whether nations with diverse populations develop more new inventions than do nations with less diverse populations. It contains graphs, charts, statistics, and quotations. Sources are listed in footnotes.	_____
3. The essay states that education helps people learn to understand other cultures. It explains three general ways that this can occur.	_____
4. The essay tells a story about a neighborhood in which ethnic groups fight because of conflicting customs. The story ends when two neighbors reach a compromise.	_____

Plan Your Essay

Use the following questions to help you make some decisions about your essay.

1. What do I want to say about the challenges of diversity in ancient or medieval Europe?

   _____

   _____

2. Do I want to tell a story, explain an idea, present evidence, or persuade others about something?

   _____

   _____

3. What type of essay will best help me accomplish my goal?

   _____

   _____

Organize Your Essay

Now that you have decided on an essay type, outline your essay. Remember to have an introductory paragraph, three body paragraphs, and a conclusion. Review how to structure each of those paragraphs. Then create your outline.

Draft Your Essay

Write your essay using the outline you created. When you're done, proofread your essay.

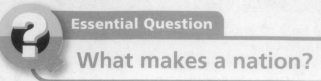

Name _____ Class _____ Date _____

? Essential Question

What makes a nation?

Preview Before you begin this chapter, think about the Essential Question. Understanding how the Essential Question connects to your life will help you understand the chapter you are about to read.

Connect to Your Life

(1) Think about foreign nations that you have visited, read about, or seen in TV shows and movies. What makes those nations different from the United States?

Things That Make Nations Different From Each Other			
Institutions	Geography	Culture	Other

Connect to the Chapter

(2) Suppose you are going to start a new nation. What are the essential things that your nation would need? Before you read the chapter, flip through every page and note the red headings, maps, and other pictures. Use your preview of the chapter to consider what you would need and record your ideas on the concept web.

What Makes a Nation?

(3) Now predict the ways that European countries have defined and expressed their nationhood. Record your ideas on the concept web using a different color pen or pencil.

(4) After reading the chapter, return to this page. Were your predictions accurate? Why or why not?

_____

_____

Name _____ Class _____ Date _____

Connect to myStory: The Battle of the Spanish Armada

1 Write a brief summary of the story about Elizabeth I and the Spanish Armada.

_____

_____

2 Record the main events of the story on the cause-and-effect chart below.

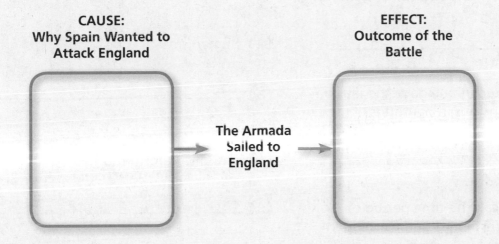

CAUSE:
Why Spain Wanted to
Attack England

EFFECT:
Outcome of the
Battle

The Armada
Sailed to
England

3 What do you think was the long-term impact of England's victory? Explain.

_____

_____

_____

Word Wise

Vocabulary Quiz Show Some quiz shows ask a question and expect the contestant to give the answer. In other shows the contestant is given an answer and must supply the question. If the blank is in the question column, write the question that would result in the answer in the answer column. If the answer is supplied, write the appropriate question.

QUESTION	ANSWER
(1) What do you call the movement that led to the formation of Protestant churches?	**(1)** _____
(2) _____	**(2)** humanism
(3) What artistic technique gave the illusion of three dimensions in paintings?	**(3)** _____
(4) _____	**(4)** Catholic Reformation
(5) What do you call the time period of renewed interest in art and learning in Europe?	**(5)** _____

Name _____ Class _____ Date _____

Take Notes

Map Skills Use the maps in *all* sections of this chapter to make a key and to
label the Places to Know on the outline map below. Remember, in addition
to this section, you will need to refer to Sections 2 through 5.

Places to Know!

Countries		Cities
England	Poland	Wittenberg
Scotland	Romania	Paris
Sweden	Belgium	London
Spain		Constantinople
Italy		Berlin

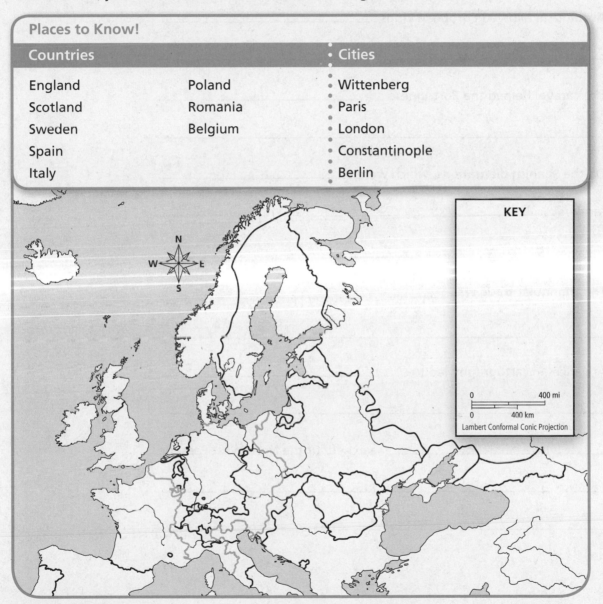

KEY

0   400 mi

0   400 km

Lambert Conformal Conic Projection

Essential Question

How might a desire to build a stronger nation affect a ruler's
decision to become a Protestant or a Catholic?

_____

_____

_____

Word Wise

Sentence Builder Complete the sentences using the information you learned in this section. Include terminal punctuation.

(1) **Absolutism** allowed European kings _____

_____

(2) The **caravel** helped the Portuguese _____

_____

(3) On the Spanish **plantations**, which were _____,

farmers _____

_____

(4) The **triangular trade** was _____

_____

(5) Advances in **cartography** led to _____

_____

(6) _____ searched for the **Northwest Passage**

because _____

_____

Name _____ Class _____ Date _____

Take Notes

Sequence Record events from the history of Europe on the timeline below.

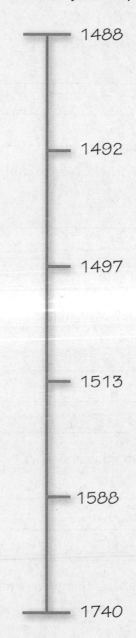

— 1488

— 1492

— 1497

— 1513

— 1588

— 1740

Essential Question

How might wars among European powers have helped build loyalty to the new nation-states?

_____

_____

_____

Word Wise

Words In Context For each question below, write an answer that shows your understanding of the boldfaced key term.

(1) What major changes took place during the **Scientific Revolution**?

_____

_____

_____

(2) During the **Enlightenment**, what methods did scholars use to study human nature?

_____

_____

_____

(3) How did the **English Bill of Rights** affect the power of English monarchs?

_____

_____

_____

(4) What event led to the start of the **French Revolution** and why?

_____

_____

_____

(5) During the **Industrial Revolution**, how did the ways things were made change?

_____

_____

_____

Name _____ Class _____ Date _____

Take Notes

Cause and Effect Use the graphic organizer below to record the causes and effects of the Scientific Revolution, the French Revolution, and the Industrial Revolution.

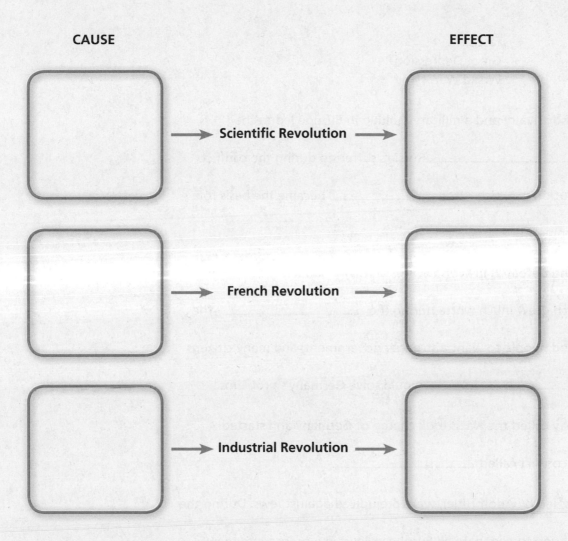

CAUSE   EFFECT

Scientific Revolution

French Revolution

Industrial Revolution

? Essential Question

How did the Napoleonic Wars encourage nationalistic feelings in Europe?

_____

_____

_____

Word Wise

Word Bank Choose one word from the word bank to fill in each blank. When you have finished, you will have a short summary of important ideas from the section.

Word Bank

communism	fascism
Holocaust	Great Depression
World War I	World War II

Nationalistic rivalry and a military buildup in Europe led to the outbreak of _____. Russia's suffering during the conflict caused a revolution in which _____ became the basis for the new government.

After being defeated in World War I, Germany had many economic problems, which grew much worse during the _____. The problems caused people to want a stronger government, and many citizens thought that _____ would solve Germany's problems.

A political party called the Nazis took charge of Germany and started another huge conflict called _____.

The Nazis, led by Adolf Hitler, were prejudiced against Jews. During the war, the Nazis tried to eliminate all European Jews in a program of mass murder called the _____. For the second time in 30 years, the Allies defeated Germany in a global war.

Name _____ Class _____ Date _____

Take Notes

Compare and Contrast In this section, you read about two world wars.
Use the Venn diagram below to describe their similarities and differences.

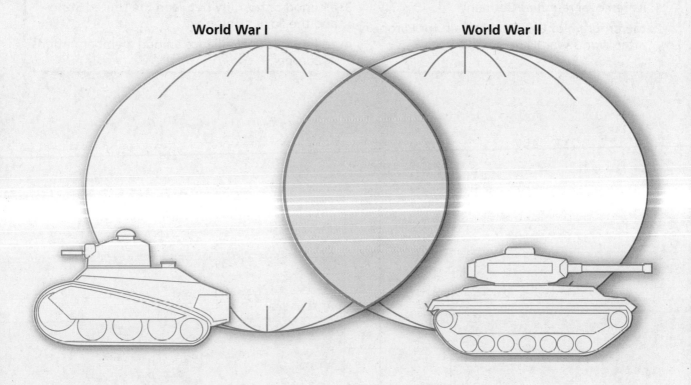

World War I   World War II

Essential Question

Why did so many nations gain independence after World War I?

_____

_____

_____

Word Wise

Crossword Puzzle The clues describe key terms from this section. Fill in the numbered *Across* boxes with the correct key terms. Then, do the same with the *Down* clues.

Across	Down
1. its removal reunited Germany	3. a period of hostility between the United States and the Soviet Union
2. the program of U.S. financial aid for Europe after World War II	4. an international alliance among member nations in Europe

Name _____ Class _____ Date _____

Take Notes

Main Ideas and Details Use what you have read in this section about Europe to complete the chart below. First, find the topic heading in the chapter. Write its main idea in your own words. Then give two details that support it.

Topic: Cold War and Division

Main idea:

Details:

1.

2.

Topic: The European Union

Main idea:

Details:

1.

2.

Topic: Democracy Spreads East

Main idea:

Details:

1.

2.

Topic: Europe Faces Challenges

Main idea:

Details:

1.

2.

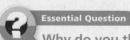 **Essential Question**

Why do you think East and West Germans still felt that they belonged to a single nation after more than 40 years apart?

_____

_____

_____

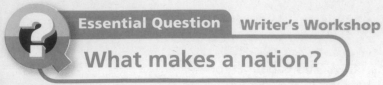

Essential Question Writer's Workshop

What makes a nation?

Prepare to Write

Throughout this chapter, you have explored the Essential Question in your text, journal, and On Assignment at myWorldGeography.com. Use these notes and what you have learned about Europe to write an essay detailing the elements that form a nation.

Workshop Skill: Use the Writing Process

Writing is a process with four different steps. However, it is not a linear process like baking a cake. You do not always have to do the steps in the same order or completely finish each step before starting the next. In writing, you can go back to earlier steps and do them over or add to what you did before. The four steps of the writing process are:

Prewrite Decide on a topic, brainstorm, gather information, take notes, and make an outline. While this is the first step, it is also one you may frequently revisit. When you are in the middle of drafting or revising, you may realize that you need to do more research.

Draft Working from your prewriting notes and outline, write the first draft of the essay. At this stage, you put your ideas into sentences and paragraphs. Remember that each paragraph needs a main idea expressed in a topic sentence. Other sentences support and explain that main idea. Use transitions to connect sentences within paragraphs and to show links between paragraphs.

Revise Reread your piece, looking for ways to improve the writing. Your goal is to make it as clear as possible. Make sure you have explained all your ideas completely. Ask yourself these questions: *Is the essay organized in the best way? Are the sentences too wordy?* Also, be sure you have used accurate nouns and active verbs. Be sure that your grammar and spelling are correct.

Present Prepare your final draft to share with others. Double space the manuscript. Include your name, the date, and the title of your piece. Again, proofread it carefully so that it is error free.

Prewrite

Let's practice the prewriting step. Review the notes you've taken and the assignments you've done related to the Essential Question, "What makes a nation?" Use the concept web below to brainstorm ideas.

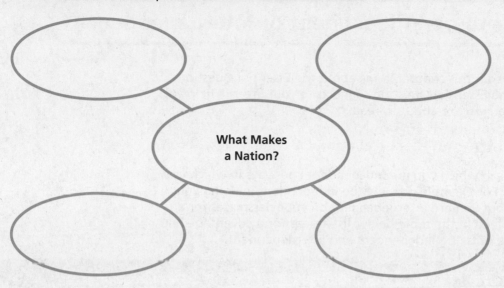

Create a Thesis Statement

Use the ideas from your concept web to write a thesis statement.

Thesis Statement _____

_____

Your thesis statement needs three supporting ideas:

1. _____

2. _____

3. _____

Draft Your Essay

Use the information you brainstormed above to write your essay on another piece of paper. You should have five paragraphs: an introduction, three body paragraphs, and a conclusion. Follow the steps in the writing process to revise, edit, and present your essay.

Name _____ Class _____ Date _____

 Essential Question

Is it better to be independent or interdependent?

Preview Before you begin this chapter, think about the Essential Question. Understanding how the Essential Question connects to your life will help you understand the chapter you are about to read.

Connect to Your Life

(1) Think about ways in which you are independent and ways in which you rely upon others. For example, you may be independent in doing your chores at home, but you are interdependent on your classmates for a school group project. In the table below, list at least one advantage and one disadvantage of being independent and interdependent.

	Advantages	Disadvantages
Independent		
Interdependent		

(2) Think of a situation in which you might act alone for part of the time and act with a group for part of the time. What are the advantages of combining independence and interdependence?

_____

_____

Connect to the Chapter

(3) Before you read the chapter, flip through every page. Note the boldfaced headings, maps, and other pictures. Try to predict areas in which European nations act independently and areas in which they act together. Record your predictions in the Venn diagram below.

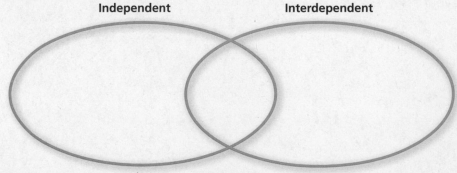

Independent   Interdependent

(4) After reading the chapter, circle your predictions that were accurate.

Name _____ Class _____ Date _____

Connect to myStory:
Europe at Her Doorstep

(1) In the table below, list the different cultures that are part of Yasmin's background. Then list details about how each culture influences her daily life.

Culture	How It Influences Yasmin

(2) How was Yasmin's family affected by Sweden's decision to join the European Union?

_____

_____

(3) How do you think other Europeans have been affected by their country's membership in the European Union? Write your predictions below.

_____

_____

_____

Word Wise

Vocabulary Quiz Show Some quiz shows ask a question and expect the contestant to give the answer. In other shows, the contestant is given an answer and must supply the question. If the blank is in the question column, write the question that would result in the answer given. If the question is supplied, write the appropriate answer.

QUESTION

(1) What is the source of the streams that flow from the Alps?

(2) _____

(3) What type of flat or gently rolling landform stretches across much of Western Europe?

(4) _____

(5) What is the name for the thick forest of coniferous trees in Northern Europe?

(6) _____

(7) What is the word for Europe's rich soil made of sediments deposited by glaciers?

ANSWER

(1) _____

(2) peninsula

(3) _____

(4) tundra

(5) _____

(6) pollution

(7) _____

Name _____ Class _____ Date _____

Take Notes

Map Skills Use the maps in your book to make a key and to label the Places to Know the outline map below.

Places to Know!

Countries	City	Physical Features
France	London	Alps
Greece		Iberian Peninsula
Italy		North Sea
Iceland		Mediterranean Sea

KEY

0 _____ 400 mi

0 _____ 400 km

Lambert Conformal Conic Projection

Essential Question

Look at the languages map in this section. Do you think the number of languages spoken by EU members helps or harms Western Europe?

_____

_____

_____

Word Wise

Word Bank Choose one word from the word bank to fill in each blank. When you have finished, you will have a short summary of important ideas from the section.

Word Bank

constitutional monarchy   gross domestic product (GDP)
cultural borrowing   Parliament
cradle-to-grave system

The United Kingdom has a queen, but the _____

actually makes all the laws. Since the government is a

_____, the queen is just a ceremonial leader. The prime

minister is the real political leader of the nation.

Scandinavian countries have a _____ in which the

governments provide benefits for people of all ages. Scandinavia is so far

north that in the summer it has a period of almost 24-hour sunlight called

the white nights season.

The United Kingdom, Ireland, and the Scandinavian countries have all

experienced increasing numbers of immigrants, which leads to

_____. The countries in these regions are generally

economically prosperous. They have a high _____, which is

the total value of all goods and services produced and sold in a nation in one

year. A country with a high GDP often has a good standard of living for most

of its citizens.

Name _____ Class _____ Date _____

Take Notes

Compare and Contrast In this section, you read about the United Kingdom and the countries of Scandinavia. Use the Venn diagram below to describe how they are similar and how they differ.

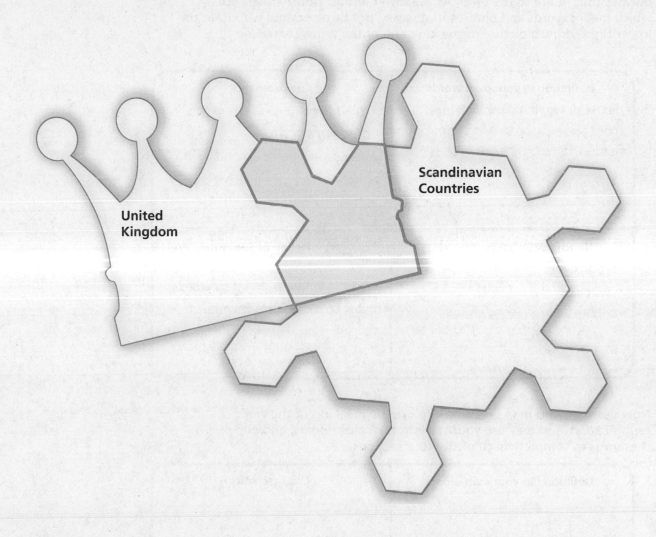

United Kingdom

Scandinavian Countries

? **Essential Question**

What are the benefits of cultural borrowing? What might be some of the challenges?

_____

_____

_____

Word Wise

Word Map Follow the model below to make a word map. The key term *polders* is in the center oval. Write the definition in your own words at the upper left. In the upper right, list Characteristics, which means words or phrases that relate to the term. At the lower left list Noncharacteristics, which means words and phrases that would not be associated with it. In the lower right, draw a picture of the key term or use it in a sentence.

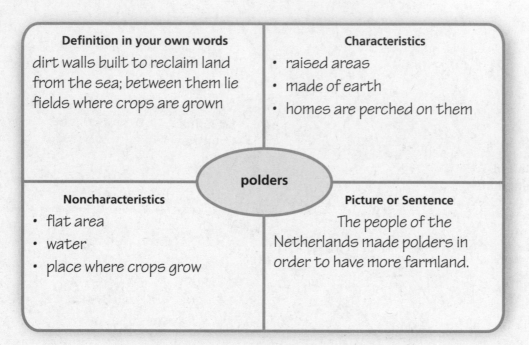

Definition in your own words
dirt walls built to reclaim land from the sea; between them lie fields where crops are grown

Characteristics
- raised areas
- made of earth
- homes are perched on them

polders

Noncharacteristics
- flat area
- water
- place where crops grow

Picture or Sentence
The people of the Netherlands made polders in order to have more farmland.

Now use the word map below to explore the meaning of the word *reunification*. You may use your student text, a dictionary, and/or a thesaurus to complete each of the four sections.

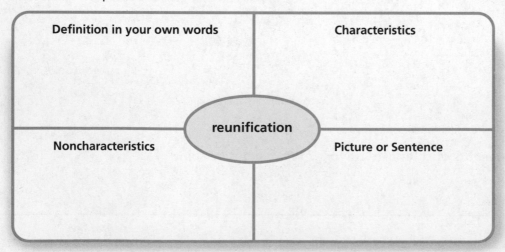

Definition in your own words

Characteristics

reunification

Noncharacteristics

Picture or Sentence

Make word maps of your own on a separate piece of paper for the following words: *privatization* and *gross national product (GNP)*.

Name _____ Class _____ Date _____

Take Notes

Main Ideas and Details In this section, you read about the countries of West Central Europe. Use the concept web below to record main ideas and details about the region's culture and international partnerships.

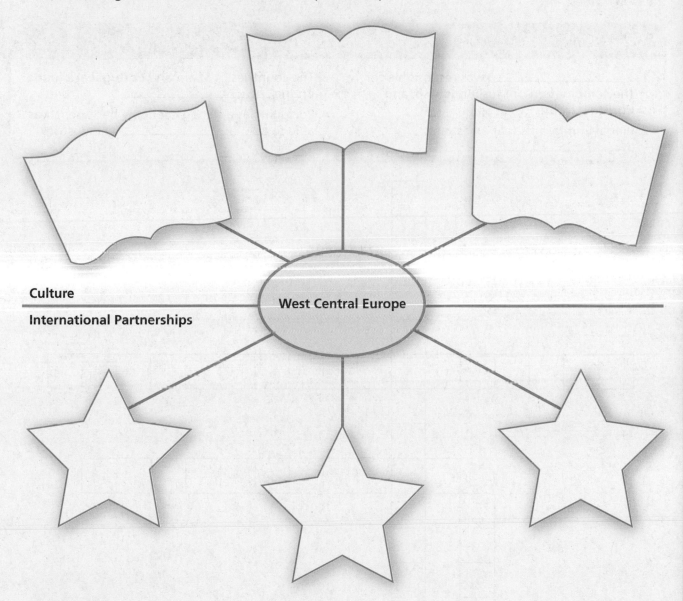

Culture

International Partnerships

West Central Europe

Essential Question

Why might EU membership appeal to smaller countries?

_____

_____

_____

Word Wise

Crossword Puzzle The clues describe key terms from this section. Fill in the numbered *Across* boxes with the correct key terms. Then, do the same with the *Down* clues.

Across	Down
1. _____ was responsible for the combination of Muslim, Jewish, and Christian influences in Spain.	3. The countries of Spain and Portugal are found on the _____.
2. Illegal immigrants fear arrest and _____.	4. Portugal has a strong economy because it was able to _____ its industries.

Name _____ Class _____ Date _____

Take Notes

Cause and Effect In this section, you read about Greece, Italy, Portugal, and Spain. Use the flowchart below to record the causes and effects of economic change and immigration in Southern Europe.

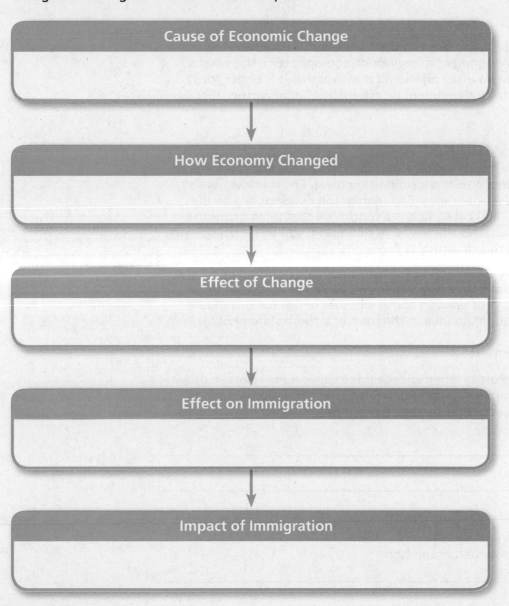

Cause of Economic Change

How Economy Changed

Effect of Change

Effect on Immigration

Impact of Immigration

Essential Question

Has the European Union helped Southern Europe? Explain why or why not.

_____

_____

_____

Essential Question **Writer's Workshop**

Is it better to be independent or interdependent?

Prepare to Write

Throughout this chapter, you have explored the Essential Question in your text, journal, and On Assignment at myWorldGeography.com. Use what you've learned to write an essay on the topic of whether it is better for European nations to stay independent or join international partnerships like the European Union.

Workshop Skill: Outline An Essay

A five-paragraph essay has an introductory paragraph that hooks the reader, states a thesis, and introduces three supporting ideas. The introduction is followed by three body paragraphs. Each paragraph develops one of the supporting ideas. The final paragraph is a conclusion that summarizes the supporting ideas and restates the thesis. In this lesson, you will learn how to outline an essay using this structure.

Identify the Main Idea Remember that a main idea is not the same thing as the topic. The topic of your essay is membership in the European Union. Your main idea will be your *opinion* about whether or not nations should join the EU. Express your main idea in the form of a thesis statement.

Write a Thesis Statement _____

Choose Supporting Points Then choose three supporting points to prove your statement. For example, if you think it is better for nations to join the EU, one supporting point might be that EU membership encourages trade.

_____

_____

Outline the Introductory Paragraph

Outline your introductory paragraph here:

Hook _____

Thesis Statement _____

Sentence Summarizing the Supporting Ideas _____

Outline Body Paragraphs

Each paragraph needs a topic sentence that states the main idea. Include evidence to support the main idea. End the paragraph with a concluding sentence that tells how the information supports your thesis statement.

Body Paragraph 1
Topic sentence

_____

_____

Supporting detail

_____

_____

Supporting detail(s)

_____

_____

Concluding sentence

_____

_____

Follow this format to write two more body paragraphs.

Outline Your Conclusion

In the conclusion, you review your thesis, summarize your supporting points, explain how those points proved your statement, and end by telling the reader why this topic matters.

Paragraph 5: Conclusion

Restate the Thesis _____

Summary of Supporting Points _____

What the Supporting Points Prove _____

Why the Topic Matters _____

Draft Your Essay

Write your essay on your own paper. When you have finished, proofread it with a partner.

Copyright © Pearson Education, Inc., or its affiliates. All Rights Reserved.

Essential Question

How can you measure success?

Preview Before you begin this chapter, think about the Essential Question. Understanding how the Essential Question connects to your life will help you understand the chapter you are about to read.

Connect to Your Life

(1) What does success mean to you? Think of some ways to measure success in the categories shown in the table below. List at least one way in each column. For example, under sports, you could list winning a major game in your favorite sport.

Measures of Personal Success			
Sports	• Arts & Drama	• Hobbies	• Relationships

(2) Think about what it takes to achieve success. Is it more difficult to reach some goals than others? Does this change the value of the success?

_____

_____

Connect to the Chapter

(3) Before you read the chapter, flip through every page and note the red headings, maps, and pictures. What factors might limit success in Eastern Europe? What factors might encourage success? Use two different colored pens or pencils to list these factors on the table below.

Measures of National Success			
Economy	• Politics	• Social Services	• Environment

(4) Read the chapter. Review the predictions you made in the table above. Circle the ones that were correct.

Name _____ Class _____ Date _____

Connect to myStory: Serhiy's Leap

(1) Think about ways that your life is like Serhiy's life. What challenges does your family face daily? How does school play a role in your life? What are your hopes for the future?

_____

_____

(2) Use this Venn diagram to compare your life with Serhiy's life. Think about family challenges, school, and hopes for the future.

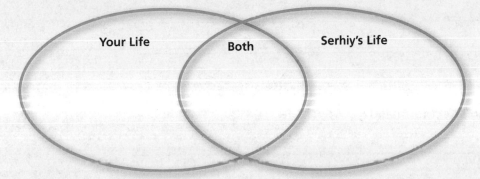

Your Life   Both   Serhiy's Life

(3) In the table below, list the challenges Serhiy faces as he tries to help his family meet its goals.

Daily Life	Making a Living	Getting an Education

(4) How do you think these challenges are affecting the people and nations of Eastern Europe?

_____

_____

_____

Word Wise

Words In Context For each question below, write an answer that shows your understanding of the boldfaced key term.

1 Why have so many Eastern European Jews chosen to **emigrate**?

_____

_____

_____

2 What happens during an **ice age**?

_____

_____

_____

3 How can **acid rain** affect farmland?

_____

_____

_____

4 What kind of land is best for **mechanized farming** and why?

_____

_____

_____

Name _____ Class _____ Date _____

Take Notes

Map Skills Use the maps in your book to make a key and to label the Places to Know on the outline map below.

Places to Know!

Physical Features	Bodies of Water	Countries
Balkan Mountains	Black Sea	Poland
North European Plain	Baltic Sea	Ukraine
Great Hungarian Plain	Danube River	Bosnia
		Herzegovina

KEY

0   200 mi

0   200 km

Lambert Conformal Conic Projection

Essential Question

To join the European Union, countries must meet certain environmental standards. Do you think protecting the environment should be one measure of a country's success? Why or why not?

_____

_____

_____

Word Wise

Vocabulary Quiz Show Some quiz shows ask a question and expect the
contestant to give the answer. In other shows, the contestant is given an
answer and must supply the question. If the blank is in the question column,
write the question that would result in the answer given. If the question is
supplied, write the appropriate answer.

QUESTION

ANSWER

(1) What do you call a person who sets up
and manages his or her own business?

(1) _____

(2) _____

(2) ethnic cleansing

(3) If one part of a country breaks away from
that country and declares itself a new
nation, what is that action called?

(3) _____

(4) _____

(4) capital

(5) What is the word for a specific style of
food?

(5) _____

Name _____ Class _____ Date _____

Take Notes

Compare and Contrast In this section, you read how different countries and parts of Eastern Europe have succeeded, while others have faced challenges. In the table below, record the successes and the challenges in each section of Eastern Europe.

	Successes	Challenges
Poland and the Baltic Nations		
Central Europe		
The Balkan Nations		
Ukraine, Belarus, and Moldova		

Essential Question

Give an example of one Eastern European nation that has been successful in recent years. Why do you think this country has been successful?

_____

_____

_____

_____

Name _____ Class _____ Date _____

How can you measure success?

Prepare to Write

Throughout this chapter, you have explored the Essential Question in your text, journal, and On Assignment at myWorldGeography.com. Use what you've learned to write a compare-and-contrast essay about how any two countries in the region have changed since the fall of the Soviet Union. Consider how each of these factors has influenced each nation's progress: physical geography and natural resources; ethnic groups; conflict/war; economic goals; and government actions.

Workshop Skill: Write an Introduction and Thesis Statement

In this lesson, you will learn more about developing a thesis and introduction for your essay. A thesis is the main point you want to make in your essay. It is neither a topic nor a title. It is an idea that you will explain in the essay. Writers generally state their thesis in the introduction. Why? The first paragraph is like an outline to your essay. It tells readers your main point and briefly lists the arguments you will make to support it.

Determine the Essay Type Think about the characteristics of the type of essay you will write. Look for signal words in the essay question. For example, the words *compare and contrast* tell you that your essay must identify and explain ways in which two countries are similar and different. This means you must give facts about both countries and then explain how the information is related.

Write a Thesis Statement Consider the main point you want to make in your essay and phrase it as a thesis statement. Here's an example: *After achieving independence from the Soviet Union, the Czech Republic had more success than Slovakia*. This statement is specific to the question and mentions two nations: the Czech Republic and Slovakia. The rest of the essay will describe the success of the Czech Republic and the success of Slovakia, discussing reasons for the different outcomes the two nations have achieved. The thesis statement may appear at the start or at the end of your introduction.

Build the Introduction An introduction tells readers what your essay will be about and why they should care about the topic. Thus, you must give readers a little background. For example, you might explain that Czechoslovakia was controlled by the Soviet Union until 1990. In 1993 it split into the Czech Republic and Slovakia. Briefly state the main points the whole essay will make. You might choose to do this with one sentence describing the overall success of one nation and then another sentence explaining the success of the other nation. Finally, tell your readers why the topic is important.

Revise Your Thesis as You Write Sometimes as you explain your arguments, you may find that they don't exactly support the thesis. You may also change your topic a little bit. Keep checking and revising your thesis as you write. For example, in the sample thesis statement, you might replace *more success* with *success more quickly*. This adds a time element to the comparison.

As you revise your thesis, remember that it must:
- fit the essay assignment
- be clearly stated and easy to understand
- be supported by facts and logic

Here is a sample thesis and introduction:

Thesis *After becoming independent from the Soviet Union, the Czech Republic achieved success more quickly than Slovakia.*

Background *Until 1990, these two nations had been the Soviet-controlled nation called Czechoslovakia. They split into two separate nations in 1993.*

Main Point 1 *Historical circumstances favored the Czech Republic. The nation's leaders also increased their advantage with aggressive modernization policies.*

Main Point 2 *The Czech Republic had a diverse economy with many different industries which allowed for rapid modernization.*

Main Point 3 *Slovakia, however, had just one main industry. When that industry slowed, it hindered the modernization of the rest of the economy.*

Why it Matters *The history of these two countries since 1993 provides lessons about why countries struggle or succeed.*

Create Your Thesis and Introduction
Now write your own thesis and introduction.

Sample thesis _____

_____

Background _____

_____

Main Point 1 _____

_____

Main Point 2 _____

_____

Why it Matters _____

_____

Draft Your Essay
Use the thesis and introduction in your essay, which will be written on another paper. Complete your essay, and proofread it with a partner.

Essential Question

What should governments do?

Preview Before you begin this chapter, think about the Essential Question. Understanding how the Essential Question connects to your life will help you understand the chapter you are about to read.

Connect to Your Life

(1) Think of different ways in which the United States government affects your life. List at least one way in each column. For example, under laws you could list laws that prohibit stealing.

How the United States Government Affects My Life				
Laws	• Taxes	• Military	• Environment	• Transportation
•	•	•	•	•
•	•	•	•	•

(2) Look at the table. Do you think the government should be doing everything you listed? Is there something that you think the government should do that it isn't doing? Write your ideas here.

_____

Connect to the Chapter

(3) Nations sometimes go through bad times such as wars or economic slowdowns. Do you think a government should take different actions during bad times than it does during good times? Record your ideas on the Venn diagram below.

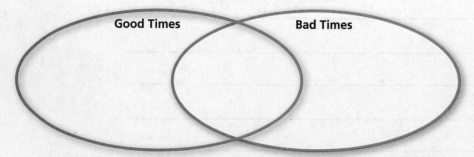

What should governments do?

Good Times   Bad Times

(4) Before you read the chapter, flip through every page and note the red headings, maps, and other pictures. Now record your predictions of what actions the Russian government will take during bad times on the Venn diagram above using a different colored ink or pencil.

(5) At the end of the chapter, come back to this page. Circle any accurate predictions you made.

Name _____ Class _____ Date _____

Connect to myStory: Boris's Bigspin

(1) Fill in the table below to compare your life to Boris's life in each of the five areas listed.

How Our Lives Compare	My Life	Boris's Life
Family		
Travel		
Social Pressure		
Sports/Hobbies		
Military Conflict		

(2) Look at what you wrote in the table above. Tell one way in which your life is easier than Boris's. Explain.

_____

_____

_____

(3) Look at the table again. Tell one way in which your life is harder than Boris's. Explain.

_____

_____

_____

(4) What does Boris's story tell you about life in Russia today?

_____

_____

_____

173

Word Wise

Word Bank Choose one word from the word bank to fill in each blank. When you have finished, you will have a short summary of important ideas from the section.

Word Bank

Ural Mountains	Siberia
Lake Baikal	steppes
permafrost	Kamchatka Peninsula

Russia is the largest nation on Earth; it stretches almost halfway around the globe! In fact, it lies on two continents: Europe and Asia. Although they are not very high, the _____ separate Russia into European Russia and Asiatic Russia. Asiatic Russia is also called _____.

Russia has large grasslands, or _____, which are where its farmland is found. One of the challenges for Russia is that that much of its soil is _____, or permanently frozen soil beneath the tundra and taiga biomes. This makes constructing roads, railroads, and buildings difficult or even impossible.

Russia has some of the most interesting geographical features in the world. There are 160 volcanoes on Russia's _____, and 29 of them are active! The nation's huge _____ holds about 20 percent of Earth's freshwater. It contains more water than the United States' five Great Lakes combined.

Name _____   Class _____   Date _____

Take Notes

Map Skills Use the maps in your book to make a key and to label the Places to Know on the outline map below.

Places to Know!	
Physical Features	**Region**
Kamchatka Peninsula	Siberia
Ural Mountains	
Lake Baikal	
Kuril Islands	

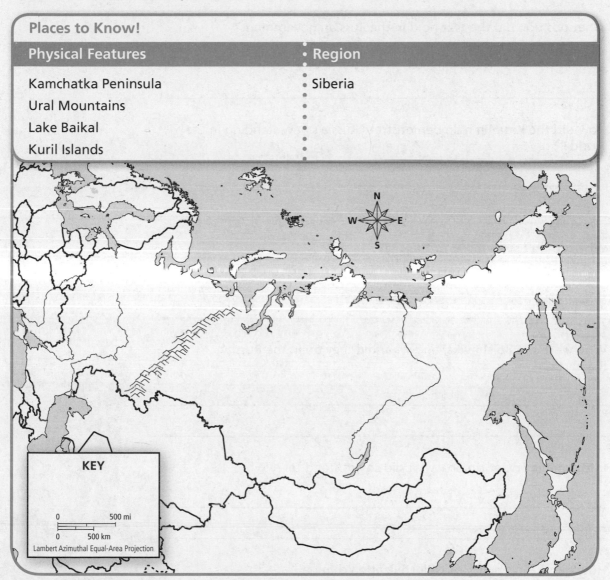

KEY

0   500 mi
0   500 km
Lambert Azimuthal Equal-Area Projection

Essential Question

Look at the railroad mileage chart in this section. The Russian government helped pay the cost of building the Trans-Siberian Railroad. Why might governments invest in transportation systems?

_____

_____

_____

Word Wise

Words in Context For each question below, write an answer that shows your understanding of the boldfaced key term.

① What position did the **tsar** hold in the Russian government?

_____

_____

② How did the **Kremlin** help demonstrate Russia's new standing in the world?

_____

_____

③ Why couldn't **serfs** move to the city?

_____

_____

④ Who were the **Bolsheviks**, and what did they do in the Russian Revolution?

_____

_____

⑤ In the name Soviet Union, what did **soviet** stand for?

_____

_____

⑥ How did Stalin's policy of **collectivization** change farming in the Soviet Union?

_____

_____

Name _____ Class _____ Date _____

Take Notes

Cause and Effect Use the cause-and-effect boxes below to record information about the Russian Revolution and the fall of the Soviet Union.

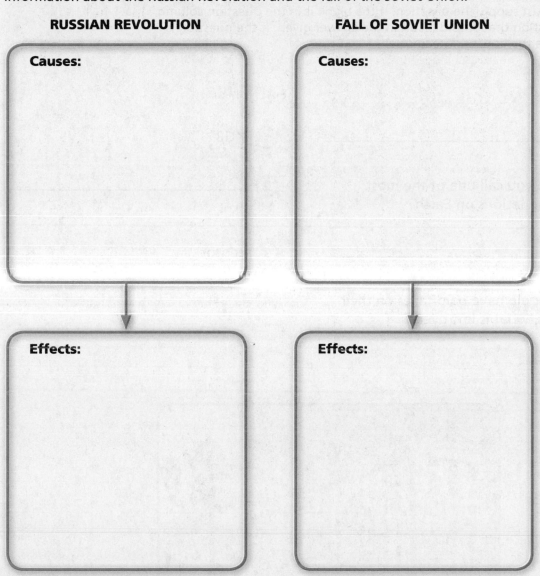

RUSSIAN REVOLUTION

Causes:

Effects:

FALL OF SOVIET UNION

Causes:

Effects:

Essential Question

Think about the famines that have occurred throughout Russian history. What actions might a government take during disasters such as famines?

_____

_____

_____

Word Wise

Vocabulary Quiz Show Some quiz shows ask a question and expect the
contestant to give the answer. In other shows, the contestant is given an
answer and must supply the question. If the blank is in the question column,
write the question that would result in the answer given. If the question is
supplied, write the appropriate answer.

QUESTION	ANSWER
① _____	① KGB
② What do you call one of the most powerful nations on Earth?	② _____
③ _____	③ censor
④ After people have paid taxes on their earnings, what is left over?	④ _____

Name _____ Class _____ Date _____

Take Notes

Main Ideas and Details In this section, you read about the many challenges faced by Russia today. Use the concept web below to record main ideas and details about those events.

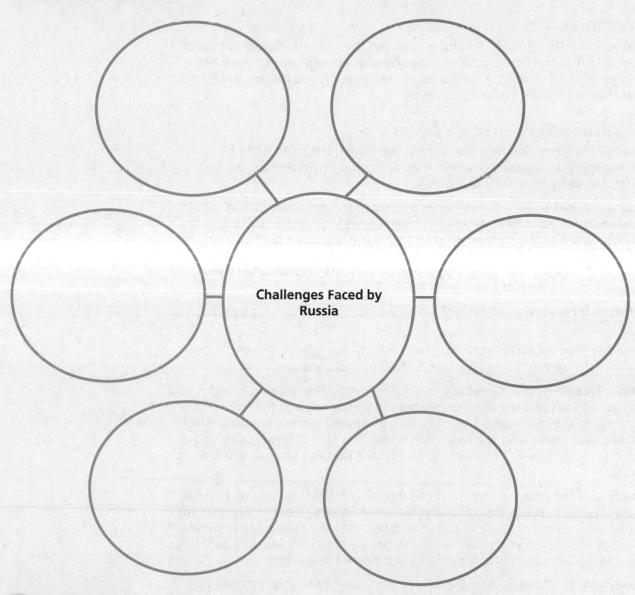

Challenges Faced by Russia

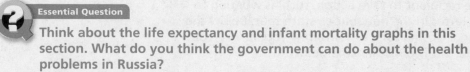

Essential Question

Think about the life expectancy and infant mortality graphs in this section. What do you think the government can do about the health problems in Russia?

_____

_____

_____

Name _____ Class _____ Date _____

What should governments do?

Prepare to Write

Throughout this chapter, you have explored the Essential Question in your text, journal, and On Assignment at myWorldGeography.com. Use what you've learned to write a formal letter stating what you believe the Russian government should do for its citizens.

Workshop Skill: Write a Letter

There are formal and informal letters. Use formal letters to write to newspapers, businesses, governments, and other institutions. Use informal letters to write to friends and family.

Today you will write a formal letter to answer the question, "What should governments do?" First, decide who will receive your letter. You might write a letter to the Russian president to another Russian politician or government official, or to the editor of a Russian newspaper. Your purpose will be to explain your ideas about what the Russian government should do.

Who will receive your letter? _____

The Parts of a Letter Your letter will include the following parts: date, heading, greeting, body, conclusion, closing, and signature.

Date, Heading, and Greeting In a formal letter, the heading includes your return address and the date in the upper right corner, and the full name and address of the recipient on the left. Skip a line and put the greeting. Most letters use "Dear" and the recipient's name. In a formal letter, use a title such as *Dr.* or *Mrs.* or *Senator* followed by the person's last name and a colon.

Body Use the body to explain your purpose. Why did you choose to write to this person? What ideas about government do you want to express? For example, you might want to state the things that the Russian government has done in recent years that helped its people. You may also discuss things that the government has done that has hindered its people.

Conclusion, Closing, and Signature Conclude by briefly restating your main point. If you want the recipient to take action, such as working to pass a law or printing your letter in the newspaper, state that. Below the conclusion, skip a line, write a closing such as "Sincerely yours," or "Yours truly," followed by a comma. Sign your full name below it.

Draft Your Letter

Use the format below to write the first draft of your letter.

(your address and date; do not put your name) _____

_____

_____

_____ **(name and address of recipient)**

_____

_____

Dear _____

Body _____

_____

_____

_____

_____

_____

Conclusion _____

_____

_____

_____

Closing _____

Your signature _____

Finalize Your Letter

Remember to follow the steps of the writing process to revise and edit your letter. Then neatly copy it onto a clean sheet of paper.

Acknowledgments

Maps

XNR Productions, Inc.

Photography

2, Mike Agliolo/Corbis; 3, Saul Loeb/AFP/Getty Images; 4, L, Bill Curtsinger/National Geographic; R, Image Makers/Getty Images; 12, Jim Sugar/Corbis; 14, Indranil Mukherjee/AFP/Getty Images; 17, Wave RF/Photolibrary; 19, Jake Rajs/Getty Images; 21, Melanie Stetson Freeman/The Christian Science Monitor/Getty Images; 23, All Canada Photos/Alamy; 27, Bruno Morandi/age Fotostock; 29, SuperStock/age Fotostock; 32, ©2008 by Ira Lippke/Newscom; 33, PCL/Alamy; 35, istockphoto; 37, LB, Pearson; 38, GoGo Images Corporation/Alamy; 42, Stephane De Sakutin/AFP/Getty Images; 43, Matthew Ward/Dorling Kindersley; 45, Todd Gipstein/Corbis; 48, Kote Rodrigo/EFE/Corbis; 49, Jeff Greenberg/PhotoEdit; 51, Andy Crawford/Dorling Kindersley, Courtesy of the University Museum of Archaeology and Anthropology, Cambridge; 52, Bettmann/Corbis; 53, O. Louis Mazzatenta/National Geographic; 55, El Comercio Newspaper, Dante Piaggio/AP Images; 57, BR, Pearson; 60, Dynamic Graphics/age Fotostock; 63, moodboard/Corbis; 67, Pearson; 68, John E Marriott/Getty Images; 70, Nathan Benn/Alamy; 77, Pearson; 82, Paul E. Rodriguez/Newscom; 83, L. Zacharie/Alamy; 88, Reuters/Enrique De La Osa (CUBA); 90, swisshippo/Fotolia; 97, Pearson; 102, Photoshot Holdings Ltd/Bruce Coleman; 103, Suraj N. Sharma/Dinodia Picture Agency; 107, Pearson; 110, *Sebastian de Benalcazar (1480–1551),* Eladio Sevilla II (fl. 1950), Oil on canvas/Museo Municipal, Quito, Ecuador/Index/The Bridgeman Art Library; 112, Steve Allen/Getty Images; 117, Pearson; 120, Reuters/Jamil Bittar; 122, Marcelo Rudini/Alamy; 128, Nick Nicholls/The British Museum/Dorling Kindersley; 132, Museum of History of Sofia, Sofia, Bulgaria/Archives Charmet/Bridgeman Art Library; 134, Geoff Dann/Dorling Kindersley; 140, Philip Gatward/Dorling Kindersley; 142, Joel W. Rogers/Corbis; 144, Getty Images/De Agostini Editore Picture Library; 146, Bettmann/Corbis; 148, Bettmann/Corbis; 153, Pearson; 166, Dean Conger/Corbis; 168, Carlos Nieto/age Fotostock; 173, Pearson; 174, Sovfoto/Eastfoto; 176, Charles & Josette Lenars/Corbis; 178, Iain Masterton/Alamy Images.